Editor
Tracy Edmunds

Editorial Project Manager
Mara Ellen Guckian

Managing Editors
Karen J. Goldfluss, M.S. ED
Ina Massler Levin, M.A.

Art Production Manager
Kevin Barnes

Cover Artist
Barb Lorseyedi

Illustrator
Kelly McMahon

Imaging
Craig Gunnell
Rosa C. See

Publisher
Mary D. Smith, M.S. Ed.

EMERGENT WRITER'S WORKSHOP

Pre•K–K

Author

Leslie Ottley, M.S. Ed.

Teacher Created Resources

Teacher Created Resources, Inc.
6421 Industry Way
Westminster, CA 92683
www.teachercreated.com

ISBN-1-4206-3224-8

©2006 Teacher Created Resources, Inc.

Made in U.S.A.

Table of Contents

Introduction

Children are naturally creative and learn very early to express themselves by drawing pictures. In fact, most children "write" before they learn to read. When guiding children through the early stages of learning to write, it is important to encourage their creativity and personal expression. *Emergent Writer's Workshop* offers tools to help implement a writing curriculum which will encourage young children to write stories incorporating new and prior knowledge. This writing curriculum is geared to students who are in preschool and kindergarten or students at similar ability levels. Children as young as three, who are just learning to hold writing implements, can benefit from the activities included in this workshop approach to writing.

It is important to keep in mind that drawing is a form of writing. For many children, their first personal narratives are drawings. Children's drawings convey their thoughts, views, and feelings about the world as they experience it. Beginning writing can consist of squiggles on a page or drawings accompanied by a string of letters or inventive spelling. To support beginning writers, you should encourage different styles of expression and offer many types of writing opportunities.

Each unit of *Emergent Writer's Workshop* begins with a song and a brainstorming activity, which are used to stimulate prior knowledge, introduce vocabulary, and suggest new ideas for writing topics. Students are also provided with a story writing page, a mini book, and a related art project.

Emergent Writer's Workshop offers students opportunities to develop writing skills while exploring a variety of interesting, age-appropriate activities and topics. Students will learn that they can write down what they are feeling and that there are many ways to write.

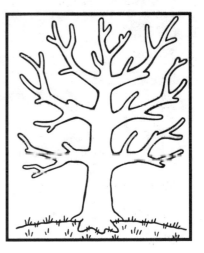

Objectives

1. Students will know that they are writers.

2. Students will know that their thoughts can be written down and shared with others.

3. Students will draw illustrations to go with their stories.

4. Students will begin to progress through the writing levels.

Encouraging Emergent Writers

We know that young writers are limited in their writing abilities — the physical act of forming letters takes practice and it takes time to develop the concentration required to sound out and spell words. Since children write about what is real to them, you should offer young writers a variety of real experiences and opportunities about which to write. Ask students to brainstorm types of writing they see in the real world and add to this list throughout the year. Listed below are some more ways to encourage emergent writers.

Generate Content and Topics for Writing

Brainstorming is a part of each unit in this curriculum and an excellent way to expand students' knowledge of a topic. Offer students opportunities to write on brainstormed topics using the Story Writing Pages and the Mini Books. Keep in mind that some young writers are intimidated when asked to write on specific topics. Some children need to be able to write on any topic they feel comfortable addressing. For this reason, the Story Writing pages for each unit are generic, except for the unit icon in the top right corner of the page. This will assist you in tracking the students' writing progress, should the pages be saved in a portfolio.

Write Daily

Establish a writing center in the classroom that is available throughout the day (see page 6). Encourage different types of writing — list making, labeling, recipe cards, story captions, poems, etc. Offer opportunities for guided writing (see page 9), including the Story Writing Page and Mini Book included in each unit. Set aside additional periods of independent writing time when students can explore in their own way.

Encouraging Emergent Writers *(cont.)*

Provide Appropriate Writing Practice

Remember that writing practice can take many forms at this age. Some students need to work on letter formation, others on spelling. Offer materials to develop fine motor skills and encourage "writing" at all levels. Try some of these hands-on activities to enhance fine motor development.

- **Play Clay**—Have play clay available to shape into letters or words. Let students use letter cookie cutters to cut out letters at random, or have them cut out their name or specific words.

- **Salt Trays**—Cover the inside of large gift box lids or baking pans with colored paper and pour in enough salt to cover the bottom. Let students write in the salt with their fingers. Students will enjoy practicing letter formation and the "writing" will be colored!

- **Index Cards**—Students can use index cards to label classroom items or write recipes for their favorite foods to create a classroom cookbook. Punch a hole in the top left corner of a series of cards and put them on a ring to create a personal picture book or word card book.

Allow Time for Thinking

Writing requires composition and transcription. It is important to remember that children need the same type of "thinking time" before writing that an adult needs. How often have you said to someone, "I just need a few minutes to think about what I want to say?"

Share Students' Writing

Students need to reread their own writing and listen to that of other writers. You will find with early writers that they are not always able to read what they have written. Encouraging students to read their own writing strengthens their understanding of the written word. Listening to and reading the writing of others widens their comprehension and helps them grasp the idea that they should be writing so that others can understand them.

Establishing an Atmosphere for Writers

As you set up your classroom, you can do many things to facilitate writing activities. Use the suggestions below to enrich the writing environment of your classroom.

The Writing Center

Stock a variety of writing and publishing implements at the writing area. Include different types, colors, and textures of paper and various writing implements such as pencils, pens, crayons, markers, or chalk. Offer index cards, envelopes, receipt pads, pencils, stamps, scissors, and tape. Change the items offered from time to time. Seasonal stickers and colored paper can be fun, too. Encourage your students to visit the writing center every day.

Bulletin Boards

Bulletin boards are a great way to publish student work. Decorate bulletin boards to reflect themes or writing skills and change the boards on a regular basis. Be certain that all students' work is celebrated.

Brainstorming Board

Place a white board, chart paper, or small chalkboard where it can be seen by all and make it a regular feature in the curriculum. Add ideas and information as each unit progresses and encourage student participation.

Reading Area

Create a comfortable, inviting reading area. Have both fiction and nonfiction books available for students. Include books on the current topic as well as seasonal favorites and books created (published) by the students. Decorate the area with theme-related pictures and posters. Change the books in the reading area on a regular basis.

Author's Chair

Establish an Author's Chair where students can sit and take turns sharing their writing with the class. This, too, is a form of publishing. The author's chair is a good way to introduce writers to the concept of "audience." It is important for students to have an audience in mind when they begin writing. For whom are they writing? Is their writing going to be read by a teacher, a family member, other students, or is it only for their personal enjoyment?

How to Use This Book

Unit Presentation

A good writing program requires preparation. Each *Emergent Writer's Workshop* thematic unit lists the materials needed and the preparation required. Patterns and templates are provided. Choose which activities the students will do each day from the unit being studied and prepare accordingly. For each unit, you will:

- Choose appropriate nonfiction (fact) and fiction books for the topic. Literature suggestions are listed on page 239.

- Copy the pocket chart cards and cut them out. Laminate them for durability and then arrange them in the correct order in a pocket chart. Please note that you will be making more than one copy of some pages—check the top of each page for directions. Punctuation cards can be found on page 240. Copy and use as needed.

- Practice singing the song ahead of time so that the tune will come easily when you sing it for the students.

- Arrange and restock the writing area. Add or subtract items for variety and change picture displays to relate to the unit theme.

- Prepare copies of the Story Writing Page for all students.

- Copy, cut out, and assemble Mini Books for all students.

- Gather materials and prepare for the art project.

Each unit is laid out in the same format, so students and teachers alike will become accustomed to the routine. As this occurs, more time will be focused on the actual writing. A typical lesson can be presented in the following manner:

Introduction

Each unit should be introduced during a group activity time. First, read a fictional story that relates to the unit topic and discuss. Then, read a nonfiction book and discuss interesting facts related to the topic.

Brainstorming

After sharing fiction and nonfiction literature, talk with students about the unit topic. Ask them to list everything they can think of about the subject. Encourage them to share prior knowledge as well as information from the books. Write student responses on a white board, chart paper, or other display board. Brainstorming improves language acquisition and comprehension and is a good opportunity for modeled and shared writing (see page 9). Explain to students that not all ideas will become part of the story, but it is a good way to share information. Brainstorming is also an excellent way to build self esteem in young children. Validate their contributions.

How to Use This Book *(cont.)*

Songs

Word cards are provided for each song. Note the number of times each page should be copied when preparing a new set of word cards. You can copy a set of punctuation cards (page 240) for use with each set of song cards or copy one set of punctuation cards to use over and over. If possible, laminate the cards. Arrange the word cards in the pocket chart. Add appropriate punctuation cards. Point out the pocket chart cards arranged in the pocket chart. Sing the song with the students (the original song lyrics are matched to a well-known tune) while pointing to each word in the pocket chart. Do this every time you sing the song to reinforce one-to-one word correspondence and left-to-right tracking. The songs will also introduce students to some vocabulary words for the unit and they can copy these words from the pocket chart when writing. Three of the songs also have picture cards illustrating key vocabulary words. You can display these in the pocket chart or place them in the writing center. Copies of the song page at the beginning of each unit can be made for students to color and take home.

Story Writing Pages

The Story Writing Pages should be completed after the books have been read, ideas have been brainstormed, and the song has been sung. Each Story Writing Page has space for a title, the student's name, and an illustration. Below the illustration area are three write-on lines for the student to write about his or her picture or for an adult to transcribe the student's dictated words. You can use these pages to do some guided writing with small groups or let the students write independently (see page 9). Some students may want to write on a different topic. That's fine, as long as they are writing!

Mini Books

Mini Books should be used later in the unit, when students have gained some knowledge of the topic. Encourage students to incorporate new information and ideas they have acquired since beginning the unit. Each book can be created with a front and back cover and two interior pages for student writing, or extra pages can be added for more experienced writers. The Mini Books are great for independent writing (see page 9).

Art Projects

Each unit includes a theme-related art project. Art projects are enjoyable for most students and offer opportunities to practice listening skills, fine motor skills, one-to-one correspondence, and other skills. Each project will require different skills and it is up to you to determine how much preparation is required by an adult and how much the students can do. It is important to have as much of the activity as possible done by the students. These projects are meant to stimulate students' writing, so encourage students to write about what they have created.

Interactive Writing Steps

Modeled Writing

When you model writing in front of the class and think aloud as you write, this is called *modeled writing*. You may be writing the daily schedule, a special note to the class, the daily news for the class newsletter, or your contribution to the brainstorming board. This type of writing demonstrates to children that there is a purpose when writing, and it allows children to observe good writing firsthand.

Shared Writing

When you encourage your students to share ideas while you do the writing, this is called *shared writing*. Usually children have some knowledge of the subject and like to contribute what they know. For example, during the dinosaur unit, you may begin by writing on a large chart in front of the class, "The word *dinosaur* means terrible lizard." Read your sentence to the class then ask, "What can I write about in the next sentence?" The children may respond by saying, "All dinosaurs hatched from eggs." You would stop at the end of the sentence and ask the children, "What goes at the end?" The children would respond by saying, "A period." The shared writing would continue until five or six complete sentences are written on the chart. You and the children can then reread these sentences together several times.

Guided Writing

During a guided writing lesson, you work with groups of children who have similar strengths and provide instruction through mini lessons. Often you model ideas and provide guidance to help these children learn the writing process, depending on the emergent and early writing levels at which the children are functioning. Children in these small groups also serve as an audience for each other's writing.

Independent Writing

Independent writing occurs when children need very little support from you. The children can work independently, writing in their Mini Books or creating original works at the writing center. Often you will show an example of the type of writing the children are expected to do. Make sure that all writing types have been introduced in previous lessons.

Tips on Transcribing Stories

Emergent Writer's Workshop was written to accommodate a broad range of skill levels (see page 11). Some children will be competent enough to illustrate and/or write their ideas with little assistance. Others will benefit from having their inventive spelling "translated." Still other children may need some coaxing to express themselves artistically or in writing.

Most young three-year-olds and students with limited speech may only say one or two words when asked about a topic or a specific illustration. To help them, expand on these shared words and make a sentence so the student can hear how a complete sentence should sound. If a student says, "my dog," say, "What is your dog doing?" The student may say, "eat." Respond with, "My dog is eating his food," while writing that sentence down on the student's paper. Repeat each sentence while writing it. Then, read the whole story back to the student when the dictation and interpretation are finished.

Some students may need coaxing to get their stories out. Ask students to describe their drawings. "Tell me about your picture." "What happens next?" If it is obviously a person, you might ask, "Who is this? Tell me about this person." With time and practice, most students will come to enjoy sharing information about their illustrations and their stories.

If a student has speech difficulties, continue to ask questions about the picture and write, to the best of your ability, what you think was said. Write in complete sentences while reading them back to the artist/author. This will help the student hear correct speech while letting him or her know that his or her words matter.

Help older four and five-year-olds who have misspelled words (inventive spelling) by writing the correct spelling above each misspelled word. Explain that you are writing the "grown-up" way of spelling the word so that others who speak the same language can read the story. Mention that sometimes a word can sound like it is spelled correctly but it doesn't look right. Words have to sound and look a certain way so that others can read them and share the meaning. This is why we learn to spell.

For students who are farther along in the writing process, invite them to read their stories aloud. Discuss interesting points and compliment them on what they have written. Use this time to help with revisions. Focus on voice, word choice, and adding details to stretch the ideas. When appropriate, ask questions. One way to do this is to focus on the senses — how did the topic of the piece look, sound, taste, feel, or smell? Some students can be taught more technical aspects of writing as well, such as correct use of punctuation, the use of spaces between words, and sentence completion. This is part of the editing process. Editing helps writers fine tune their pieces to make them better. Authors can revise pieces many times to get them just right, which is part of the process of writing.

Assessing Emergent Writers

Emergent Writing Stages

In order to assess where students are and where they are going in their writing progression, you need to understand how children naturally develop their writing skills. Developmentally, children come to understand writing as they progress through the following stages:

- I can think about something.
- I can talk about what I think.
- I can write about what I say.
- I can read what I write.
- Other people can read what I write, too.
- I can affect the way other people think about things.

Emergent Writing Levels

At each developmental stage, students gain new writing skills and abilities. When you know what students' current emergent writing skills are, you can provide appropriate writing opportunities and practice to expand those skills. The following rubric identifies the five levels of emergent writing skills. At the end of each unit, assess each student's Story Writing Page and assign a current level to the writer. Keep the Story Writing Pages in a folder and review them often. By looking at how students' writing changes over time, you will be able, through modeled, writing (page 9), to guide them to the next levels. Examples of student work at each of these levels can be found on pages 12–21.

Rubric

- ✎ **Pre-Writer**—The student draws pictures which may or may not be recognizable. The student writes with scribble writing and letter-like figures.

- ✎ **Beginning Writer**—The student draws recognizable pictures that are relevant to the topic. The student understands that print conveys meaning. The student writes one, two, or three letter combinations to represent whole words, using mostly uppercase letters.

- ✎ **Developing Writer**—The student uses pictures and print to convey meaning. The student copies names and words. The student is beginning to use some letter/sound relationships to write unfamiliar words, especially for the beginning and ending sounds. The student adds labels.

- ✎ **Proficient Writer**—The student writes common words based on letter-sound relationships. The student may still confuse some letter sounds. The student uses both upper and lowercase letters in writing. The student writes left to right and top to bottom. The student uses appropriate spacing. The student writes complete thoughts.

- ✎ **Expert Writer**—The student spells high frequency words correctly and uses knowledge of some word patterns to spell words correctly. The student uses developmental spelling with unfamiliar words. The student is starting to use punctuation and captialization. The student spaces words appropriately. The student stays on the topic and writes multiple sentences. The student begins to write sentences with purposeful order.

Pre-Writer

Translation:

This snowman is melting.

by Maycie

Pre-Writer

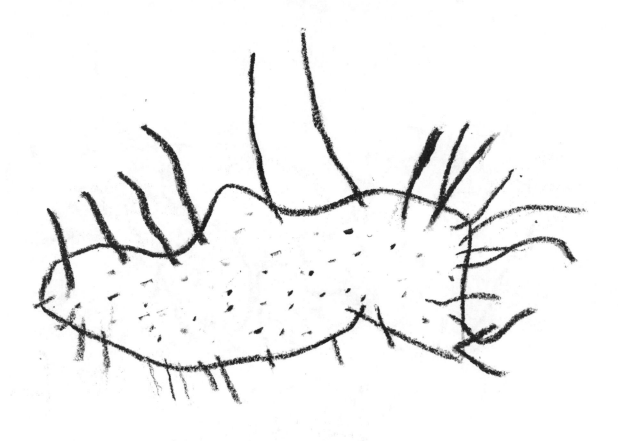

Translation:

A lion with chicken pox and lots
of legs is running after my daddy.

by Lucas

Beginning Writer

10pcs leesje

Translation:

I saw a snowman alive. He kissed me.

by Jessica

Beginning Writer

WUZABQR

Translation:

There was a bear.

by Sarah

Developing Writer

Translation:

cat   hen   tree

Developing Writer

Translation:

My sister stuck her feet in the water.
She got stickers in her feet.

by Madison

Proficient Writer

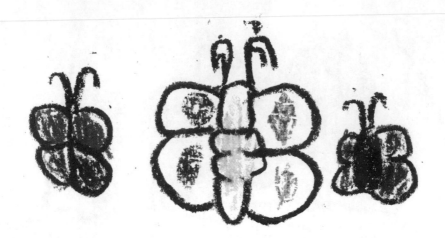

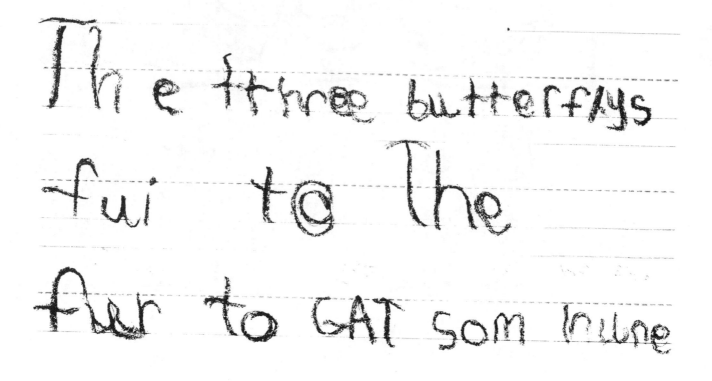

The ttrhee butterflys
fui to The
fler to GAT som huune

Translation:

The three butterflies fly to
the flower to get some honey.

by Jade

Proficient Writer

Ouns ther wrere
a jinjrbred famule
ther wus a man a
woman and a babee

Translation:

Once there were a gingerbread family.
There was a man, a woman, and a baby.

by Shelby

Expert Writer

Translation:

The three ladybugs were flying
to the leaf to get some milk.

by Kandace

Expert Writer

I like my kitten.
She is nice. I like
to play with mykit
en.

Translation:

> I like my kitten. She is nice.
> I like to play with my kitten.

by Kori

Writing Standards

In addition to the Emergent Writing Stages and Levels (pages 11–21), you can use Writing Standards to evaluate students' progress. Some students will be able to master all of these standards, while other students will just begin to incorporate some of these skills into their writing. The standards listed in the following categories are to be met by the end of the year, not the beginning.

Standards for the End of Preschool

1. Shares ideas for class writing.

2. Organizes ideas through group discussion (with teacher assistance).

3. Draws identifiable pictures.

4. Shares drawings with others.

5. Dictates words, phrases, or sentences to an adult.

6. Dictates a title that matches the topic.

7. Writes using strings of letters.

Standards for the End of Kindergarten

1. Selects ideas for writing (with teacher assistance).

2. Organizes and sequences ideas for a story (with teacher assistance).

3. Draws or writes simple stories with teacher assistance.

4. Shares drawings or writing with others.

5. Draws detailed, identifiable pictures.

6. Writes to go along with drawings.

7. Writes a title that matches the topic.

8. Puts letters together to form words and sentences.

Fall

(Sing to the tune of "Twinkle, Twinkle Little Star")

Red and yellow, orange and brown.

Leaves are changing all around.

Soon they will fall to the ground,

Flutter, flutter, flutter down.

Red and yellow, orange and brown,

Leaves are changing all around.

Fall Lesson Plan

Unit Materials

- age-appropriate fiction and nonfiction books about fall
- white board or chart paper and markers
- Fall Song Pocket Chart Cards (pages 30–34) laminated and cut apart
- pocket chart
- markers, colored pencils, and crayons
- Fall Story Writing Page for each child (page 25)
- assembled Fall Mini Book for each student (pages 26–28)
- Fall Tree Pattern (page 29) and project materials (page 26) for each student

Fall

Leaves

Flutter

Unit Introduction

1. Read a fictional story about fall. Discuss the setting, characters, and plot.

2. Share a nonfiction book about fall, pointing out interesting facts.

3. Brainstorm. Write *Fall* at the top of a chart or white board. Ask students to share what they know about fall time and write down their responses. Use the shared writing technique detailed on page 9.

4. Sing the *Fall* song while pointing to each of the words on the pocket chart.

5. Pass out the Story Writing Page. Encourage students to write or draw their own stories about fall. You can use this time to do some guided writing with small groups or have the children write independently (see page 9).

6. Spend time with each child discussing his or her story or illustration. You will find tips for transcribing and editing students' stories on page 10.

Unit Activities

1. Continue sharing the fiction book about fall that you read during the unit introduction. Reread the nonfiction book and discuss interesting facts. Introduce additional books about fall during the week.

2. Add student ideas and new facts about fall to the brainstorming board.

3. Continue singing the Fall song, pointing to the cards in the pocket chart each time. Remind students that they can use these words in their writing.

4. Use the Fall Mini Book (pages 26–28) for guided or independent writing (see page 9). Encourage students to incorporate new information and ideas they have acquired since beginning the unit.

5. Complete the Fall Tree Art Project (pages 26 and 29), display them in the classroom, and encourage students to write about their work.

My Story About _____

By _____

Fall Mini Book

Materials

- Fall Mini Book patterns (pages 27 and 28)
- brown, red, or gold construction paper
- white paper
- scissors
- stapler

Assembly Directions

1. Copy pages 27 and 28 (one of each page per student) onto brown, red, or gold construction paper, and cut out the leaf shapes to create the front and back covers of the Fall Mini Books.

2. Make copies of the leaf pattern (page 28) on white paper and cut them out to make the inside pages of the mini books. For early writers, two pages per book will probably be sufficient. For more experienced writers, increase the number of pages.

3. Assemble the books and staple them together.

Fall Tree Art Project

Materials

- Fall Tree Art Pattern (page 29)
- fall colored (gold, brown, red, orange, etc.) tissue paper cut into squares
- white glue
- small, shallow lids or cups for glue
- pencils
- crayons, colored pencils, or markers

Preparation

- Make copies of the Fall Tree Art Pattern (one per student).
- Put a blob of glue into each lid or cup.

Assembly Directions

1. Have students color their tree trunks brown.

2. Show students how to twist a piece of tissue paper around the eraser end of a pencil, dip it into the glue, and stick it on the tree.

3. Let students cover their trees with fall leaves.

4. Display students' trees in the classroom and encourage students to write about their work.

Fall Mini Book

Cover

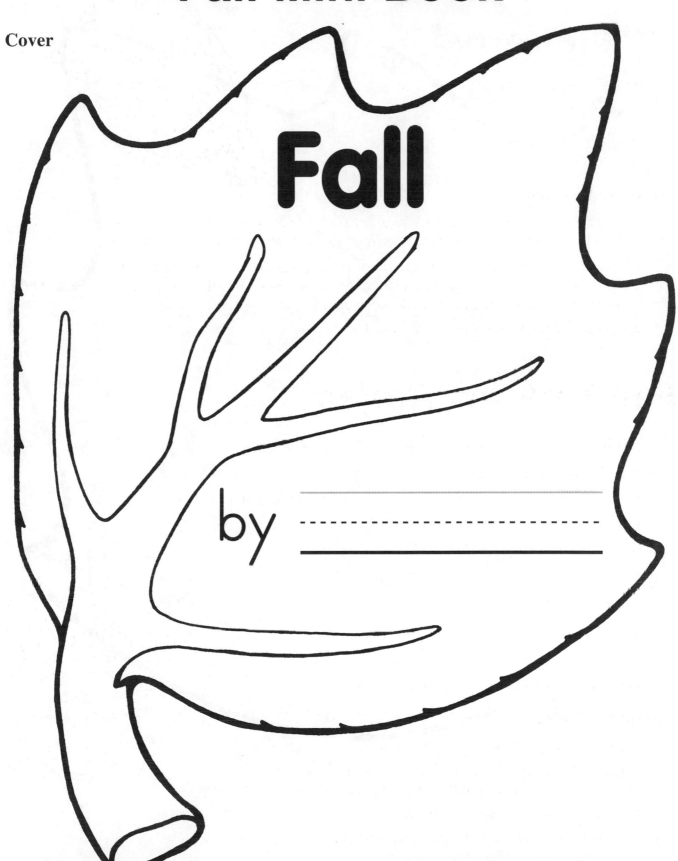

Fall

by _____

Fall Mini Book *(cont.)*

Back Cover and Inside Pages

Fall Tree Art

Pattern

Make **two** copies of this page. **Note:** The "Fall" title card is used only once.

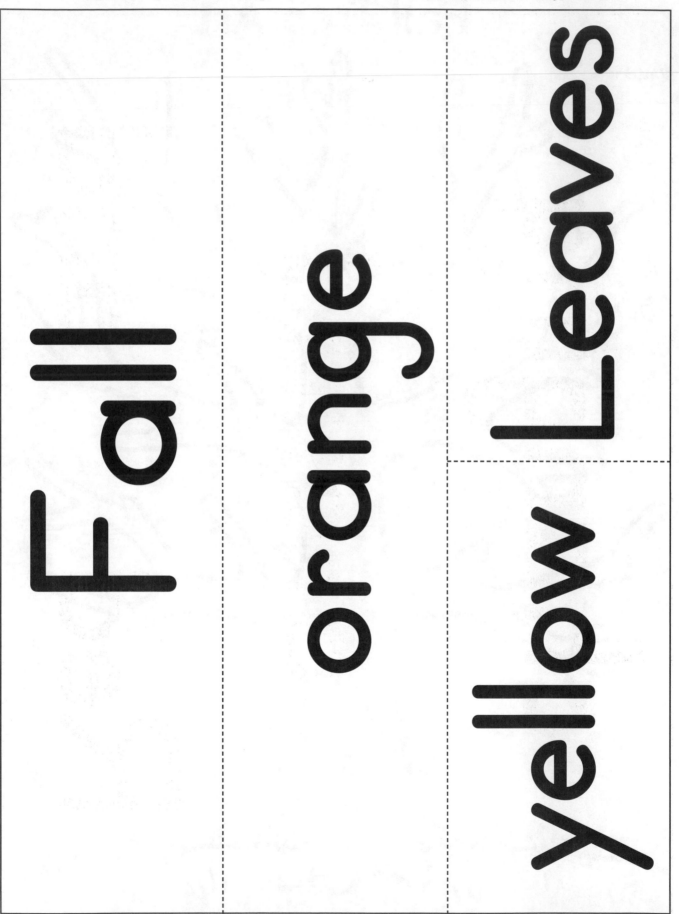

Make **two** copies of this page.

changing

around

and

Red

Make **two** copies of this page. Note: The "ground" and "down" cards are only used once.

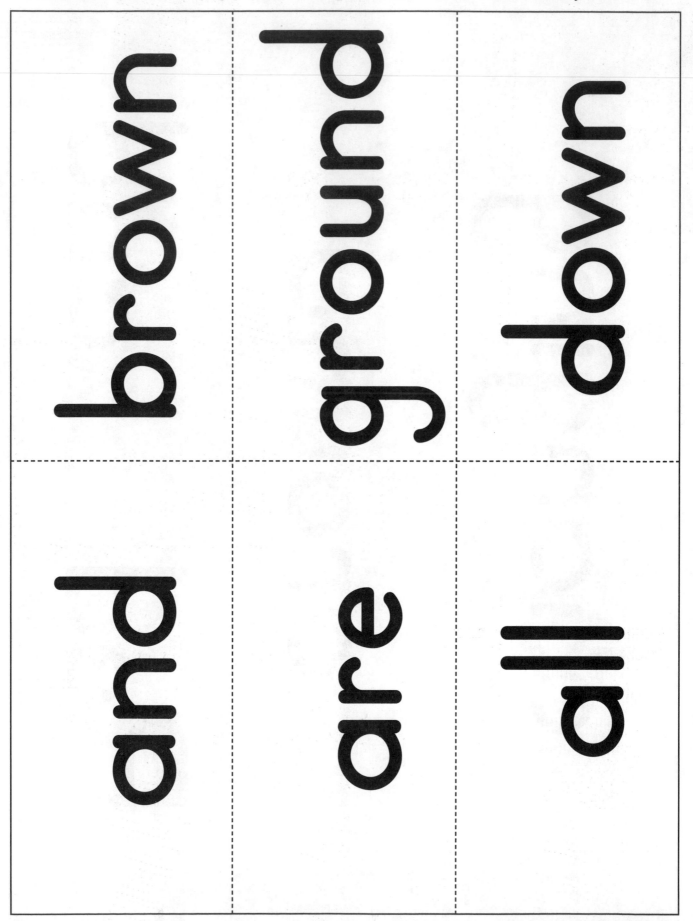

Make **one** copy of this page.

they

fall

the

Soon

will

to

Make **one** copy of this page.

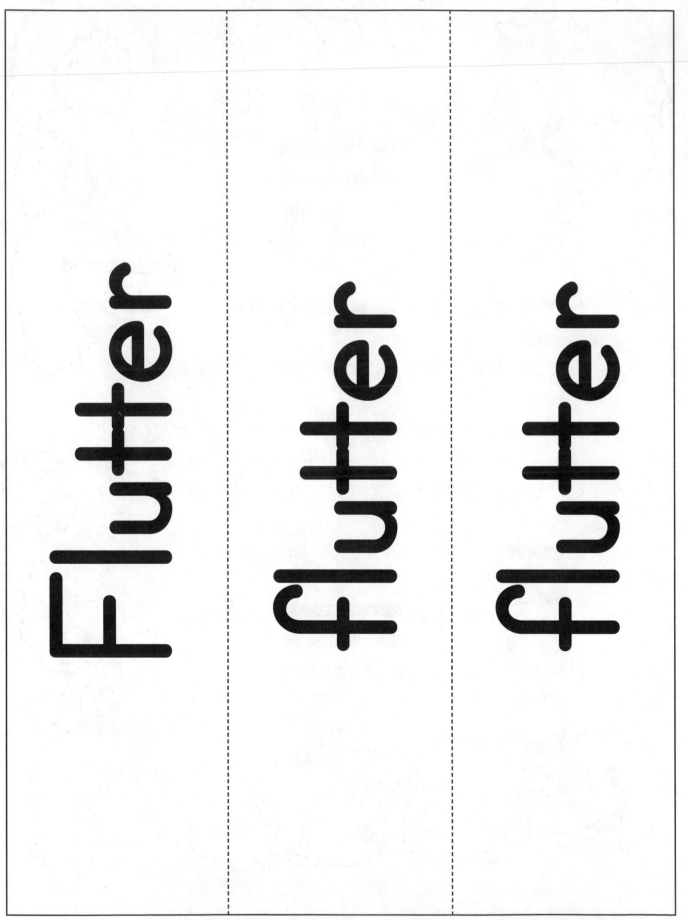

About Me

(Sing to the tune of "Up on the House Top")

I am special, can't you see?

I am the one and only me.

I can be nice and share my toys,

I have friends, both girls and boys.

Grow, grow, grow, don't you know,

Ho, ho, ho, watch me grow!

I'm getting bigger every day,

I'm so special in every way.

About Me

Materials

- age-appropriate fiction and nonfiction books about children and how they are alike and different from each other

- white board or chart paper and markers

- About Me Pocket Chart Cards (pages 42–50) laminated and cut apart

- pocket chart

- markers, colored pencils, and crayons

- About Me Story Writing Page for each child (page 37)

- assembled About Me Mini Book for each student (pages 38–40)

- Self Portrait Pattern (page 41) and project materials (page 38) for each student

Unit Introduction

1. Read a fictional story about children. Discuss the setting, characters, and plot.

2. Share a nonfiction book about children, pointing out interesting facts.

3. Brainstorm. Write *About Me* at the top of a chart or white board. Ask students to share how they are the same or different and their likes or dislikes and write down their responses. Use the shared writing technique detailed on page 9.

4. Sing the About Me song while pointing to each of the words on the pocket chart.

5. Pass out the Story Writing Page. Encourage students to write or draw their own stories about themselves. You can use this time to do some guided writing with small groups or have the children write independently (see page 9).

6. Spend time with each child discussing his or her story or illustration. You will find tips for transcribing and editing students' stories on page 10.

Unit Activities

1. Continue sharing the fiction book about children that you read during the unit introduction. Reread the nonfiction book and discuss interesting facts. Introduce additional books about children during the week.

2. Add student ideas and new facts about themselves to the brainstorming board.

3. Continue singing the About Me song, pointing to the cards in the pocket chart each time. Remind students that they can use these words in their writing.

4. Use the About Me Mini Book (pages 38–40) for guided or independent writing (see page 9). Encourage students to incorporate new information and ideas they have acquired since beginning the unit.

5. Complete the Self Portrait Art Project (pages 38 and 41), display them in the classroom, and encourage students to write about their work.

My Story About _____

By _____

About Me Mini Book

Materials

- About Me Mini Book book patterns (pages 39–40)
- colored construction paper
- white paper
- scissors
- stapler

Assembly Directions

1. Copy pages 39 and 40 (one of each page per student) onto colored construction paper and cut out the body shapes to create the front and back covers of the About Me Mini Books.

2. Make copies of the body pattern (page 40) on white paper and cut them out to make the inside pages of the mini books. For early writers, two pages per book will probably be sufficient. For more experienced writers, increase the number of pages.

3. Assemble the books and staple them together.

Self Portrait Art Project

Materials

- Self Portrait Patterns (page 41) on heavy white paper
- paints in skintone colors
- crayons
- brown, black, red, and yellow yarn
- scissors
- glue or paste

Preparation

- Make copies of the Self Portrait Pattern (one for each student).
- Cut different lengths of yarn for hair.
- Prepare for painting.

Assembly Directions

1. Have students draw facial features (eyes, nose, mouth) on their Self Portrait Patterns with crayons. Remind them to make their portraits look as similar to their own faces as possible.

2. Have students paint their portraits to resemble their own skin colors.

3. Let students select and glue on the color and length of yarn that best matches their own hair.

4. Hang the students' self portraits in the classroom and encourage them to write autobiographies.

About Me Mini Book

Cover

About Me Mini Book *(cont.)*

Back Cover and Inside Pages

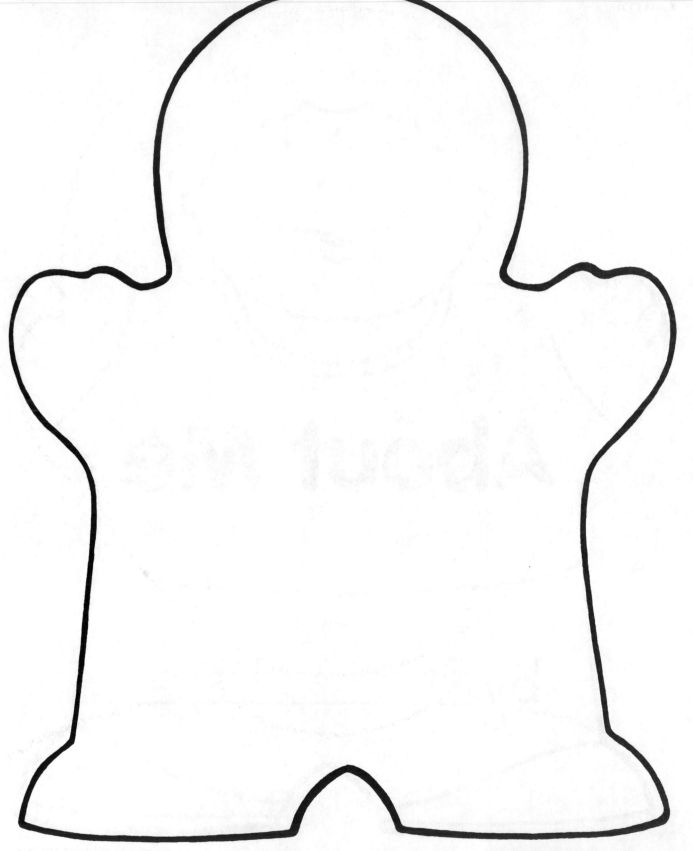

Self Portrait

Pattern

Make **one** copy of this page.

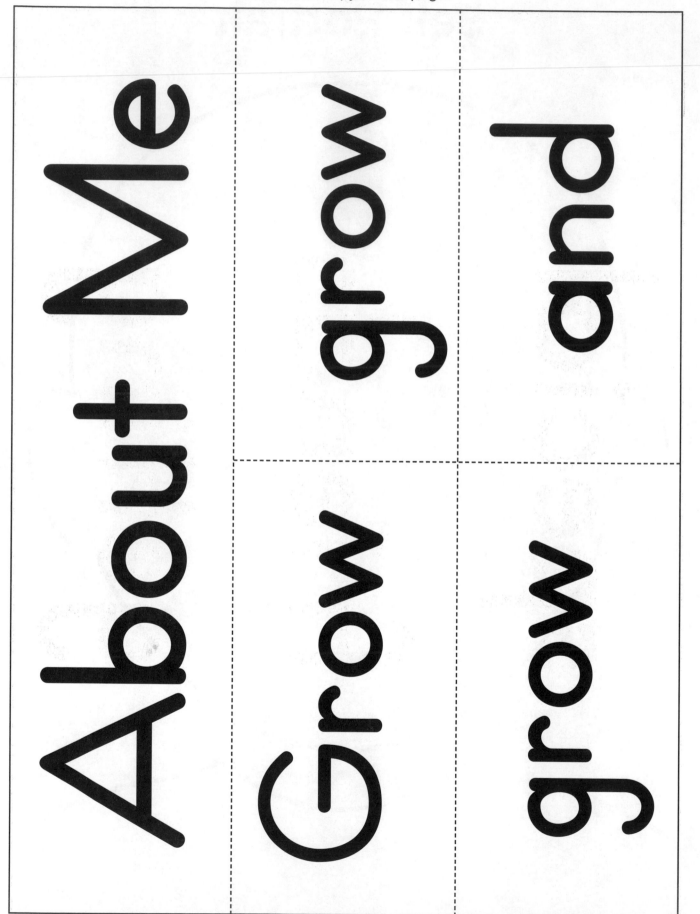

Make **one** copy of this page.

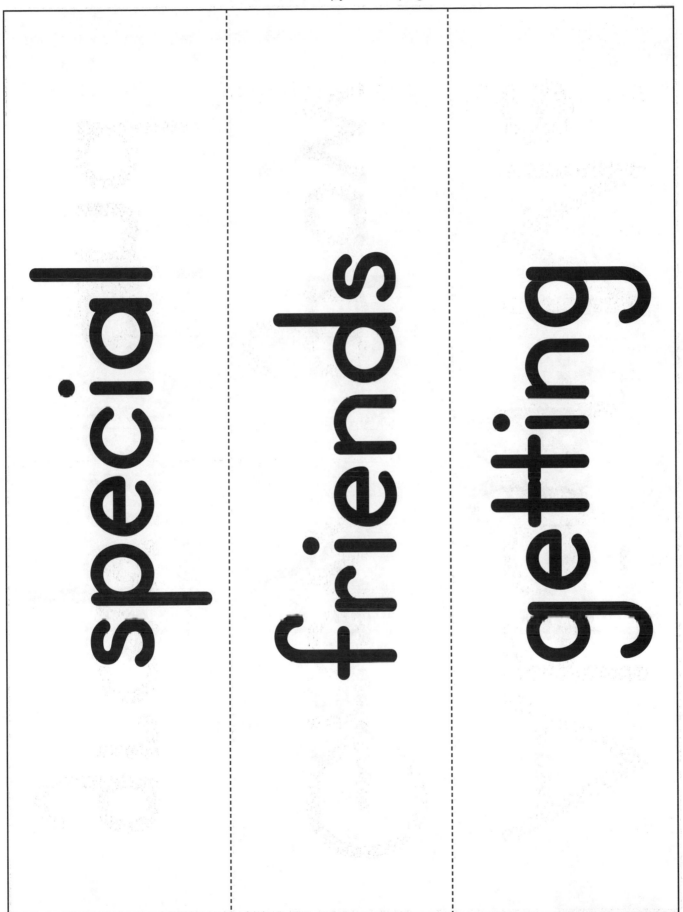

special

friends

getting

Make **one** copy of this page.

bigger

day

every

special

44

Make **one** copy of this page.

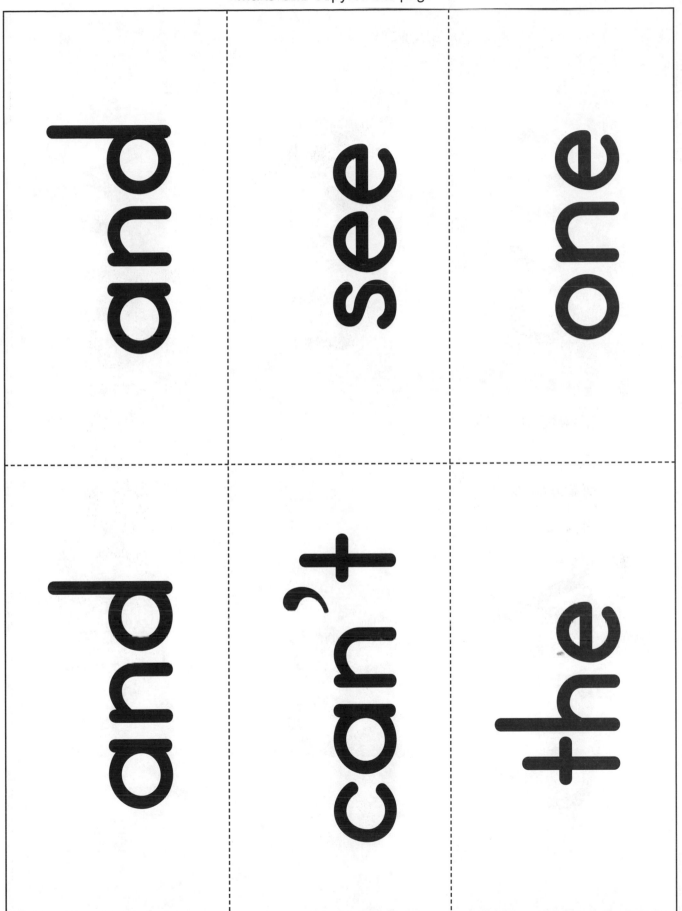

Make **one** copy of this page.

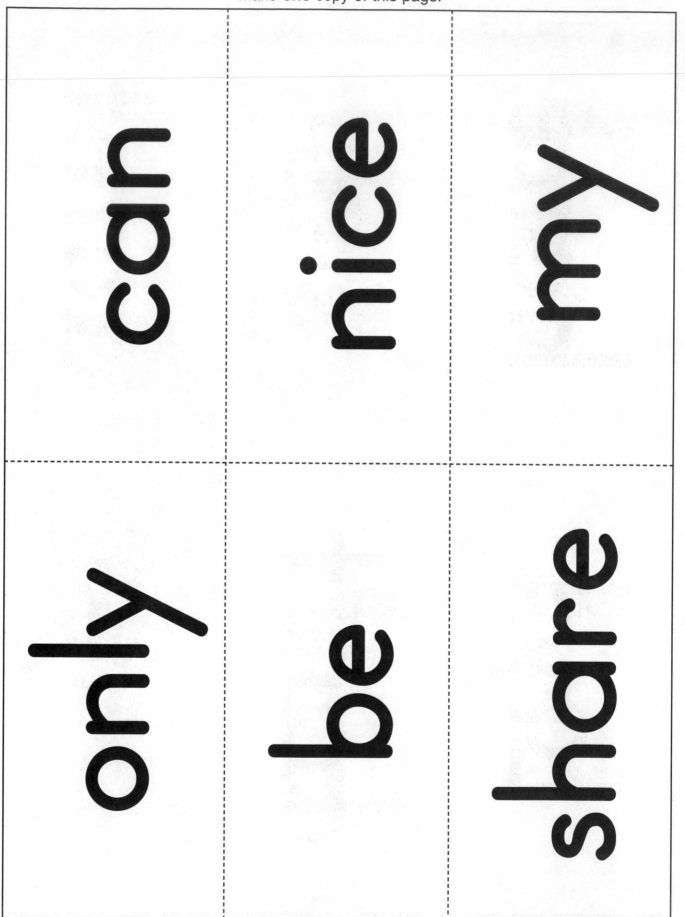

Make **one** copy of this page.

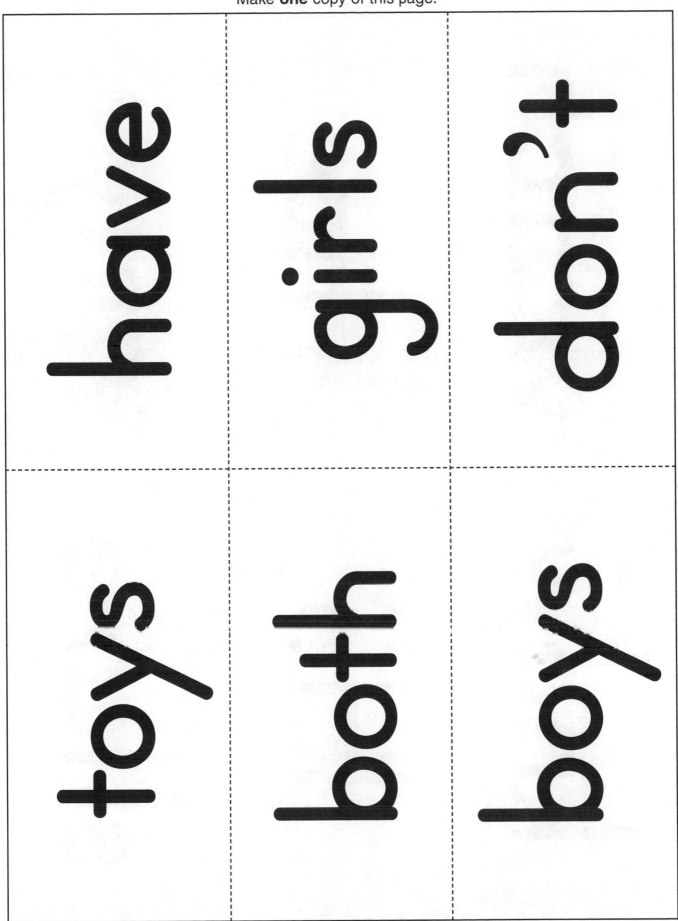

have

girls

don't

toys

both

boys

Make **one** copy of this page.

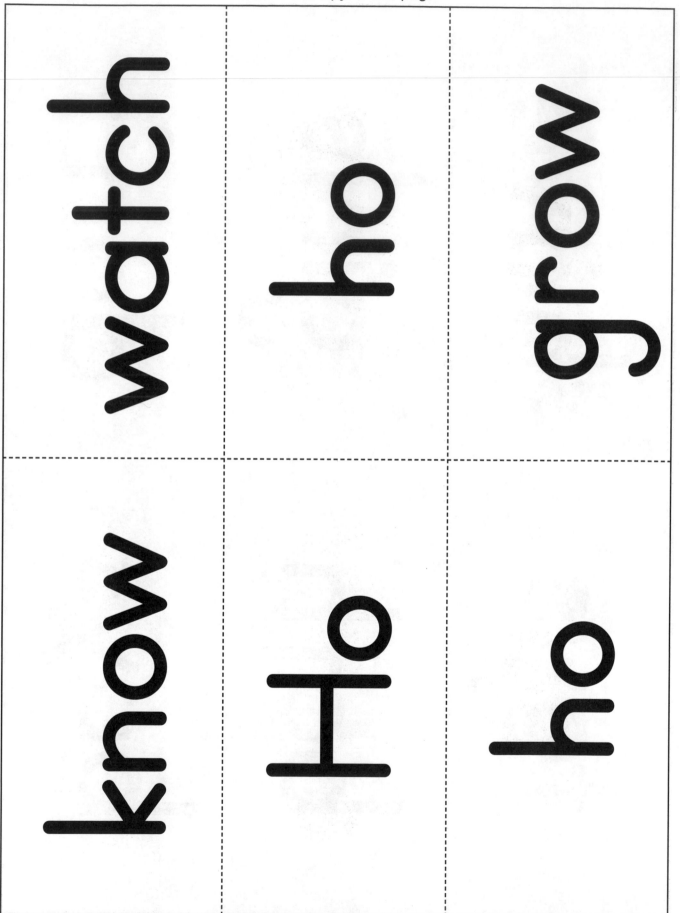

watch

ho

grow

know

Ho

ho

Make **one** copy of this page.

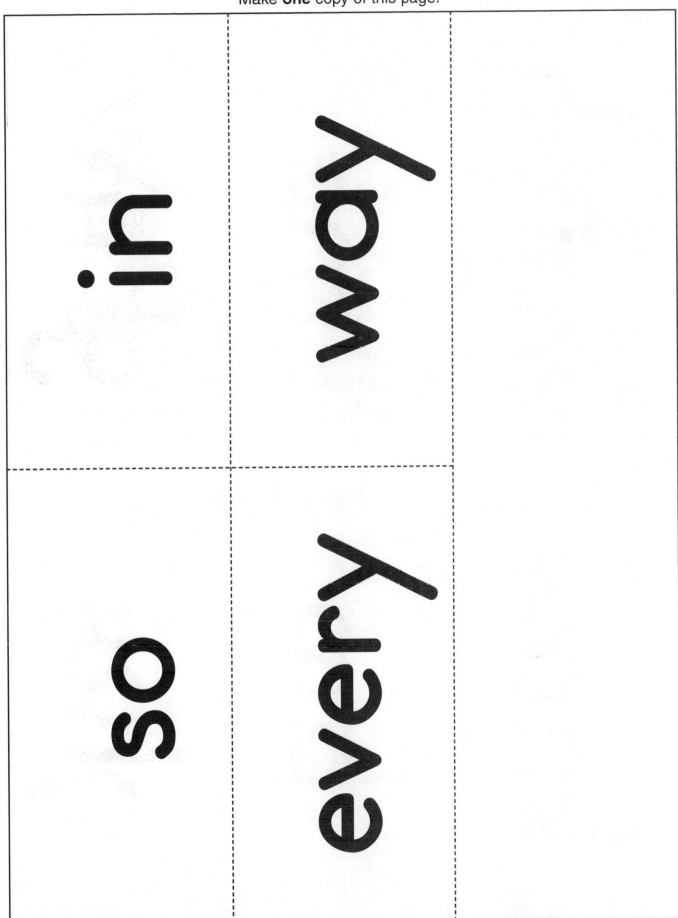

in

way

so

every

Make **two** copies of this page.

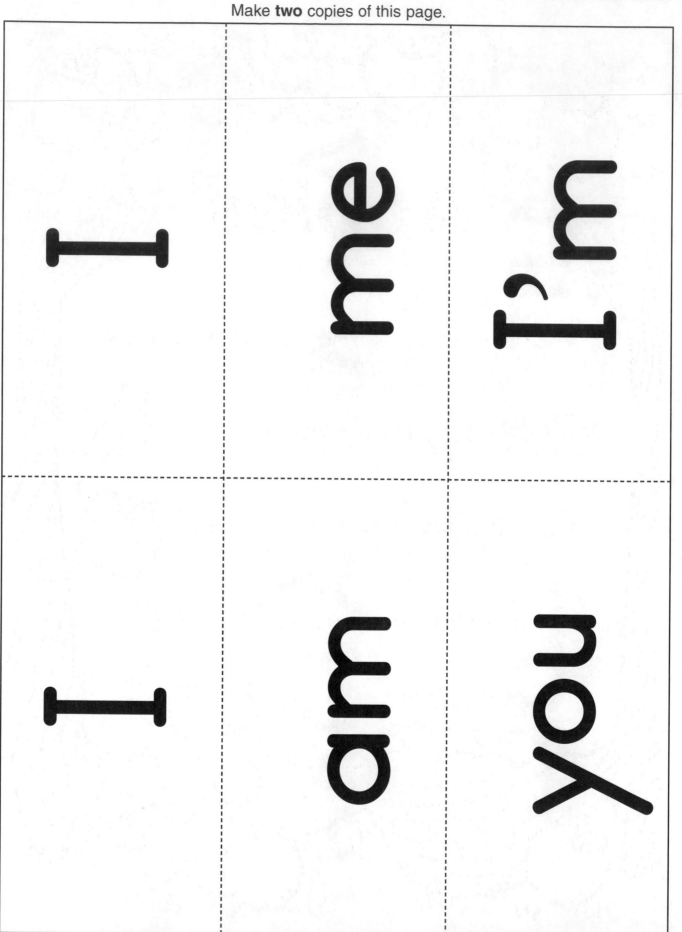

Apples

(Sing to the tune of "My Bonnie Lies Over the Ocean")

Apples, they come in three colors,

Red is so yummy to me,

Green can be ever so sour,

And yellow is sweet as can be.

Apples

Red

Green

Yellow

Materials

- age-appropriate fiction and nonfiction books about apples
- white board or chart paper and markers
- Apples Song Pocket Chart Cards (pages 58–62) laminated and cut apart
- pocket chart
- markers, colored pencils, and crayons
- Apples Story Writing Page for each child (page 53)
- assembled Apple Mini Book for each student (pages 54–56)
- Apple Art Pattern (page 57) and project materials (page 54) for each student

Unit Introduction

1. Read a fictional story about apples. Discuss the setting, characters, and plot.

2. Share a nonfiction book about apples, pointing out interesting facts.

3. Brainstorm. Write *Apples* at the top of a chart or white board. Ask students to share what they know about apples and write down their responses. Use the shared writing technique detailed on page 9.

4. Sing the Apples song while pointing to each of the words on the pocket chart.

5. Pass out the Story Writing Page. Encourage students to write or draw their own stories about apples. You can use this time to do some guided writing with small groups or have the children write independently (see page 9).

6. Spend time with each child discussing his or her story or illustration. You will find tips for transcribing and editing students' stories on page 10.

Unit Activities

1. Continue sharing the fiction book about apples that you read during the unit introduction. Reread the nonfiction book and discuss interesting facts. Introduce additional books about apples during the week.

2. Add student ideas and new facts about apples to the brainstorming board.

3. Continue singing the Apples song, pointing to the cards in the pocket chart each time. Remind students that they can use these words in their writing.

4. Use the Apple Mini Book (pages 54–56) for guided or independent writing (see page 9). Encourage students to incorporate new information and ideas they have acquired since beginning the unit.

5. Complete the Apple Art Project (pages 54 and 57), display them in the classroom, and encourage students to write about their work.

My Story About _____

By _____

Apple Mini Book

Materials

- Apple Mini Book patterns (pages 55 and 56)
- red, yellow, or green construction paper
- white paper
- scissors
- stapler

Assembly Directions

1. Copy pages 55 and 56 (one of each page per student) onto red, yellow, or green construction paper and cut out the apple shapes to create the front and back covers of the Apple Mini Books.

2. Make copies of the apple pattern (page 56) on white paper and cut them out to make the inside pages of the mini books. For early writers, two pages per book will probably be sufficient. For more experienced writers, increase the number of pages.

3. Assemble the books and staple them together.

Apple Wreath

Materials

- paper plates
- Apple Art Patterns (page 57)
- red, yellow, and green construction paper
- scissors
- glue or paste
- string or chenille stick
- hole punch

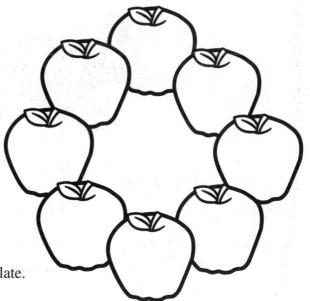

Preparation

- Make copies of the Apple Art Patterns on red, yellow, and green construction paper.
- Cut a 5" (13 cm) hole in the center of each paper plate.
- Punch a hole in the top of each plate for hanging.

Assembly Directions

1. Give each student a prepared paper plate wreath shape.

2. Have each student cut out red, yellow, and green apples.

3. Have students paste the apples around the edge of the paper plate. They can paste them randomly or make a pattern with the three colors.

4. Attach a string or chenille stick loop to the hole in the top of each plate and display students' apple wreaths in the classroom. Encourage students to write about their art work.

Apple Mini Book

Apples

by _____

Apple Mini Book *(cont.)*

Back Cover and Inside Pages

Apple Art

Patterns

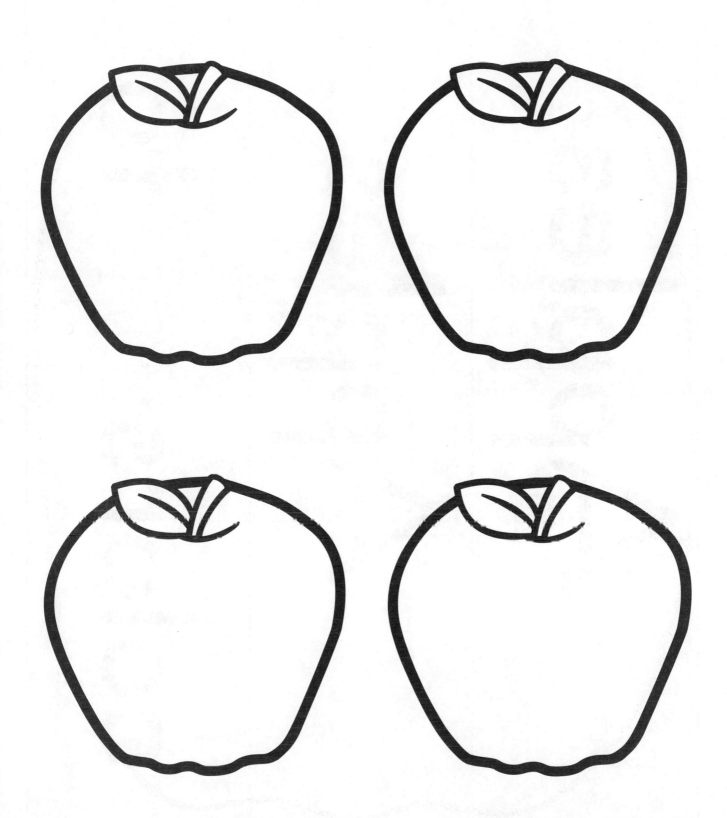

Make **one** copy of this page.

Apples

Apples

to

colors

Make **one** copy of this page.

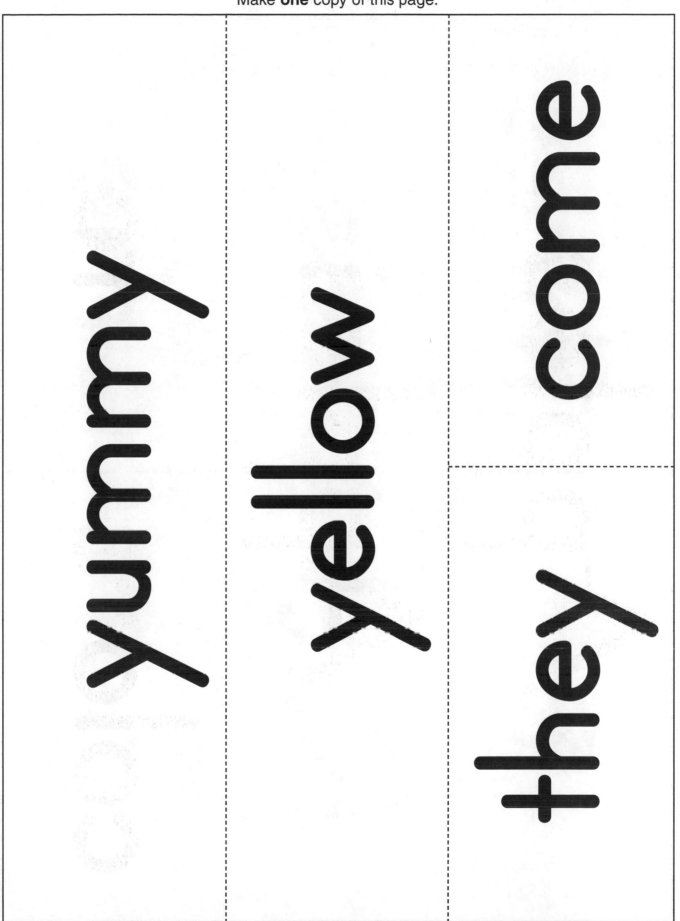

yummy

yellow

come

they

Make **one** copy of this page.

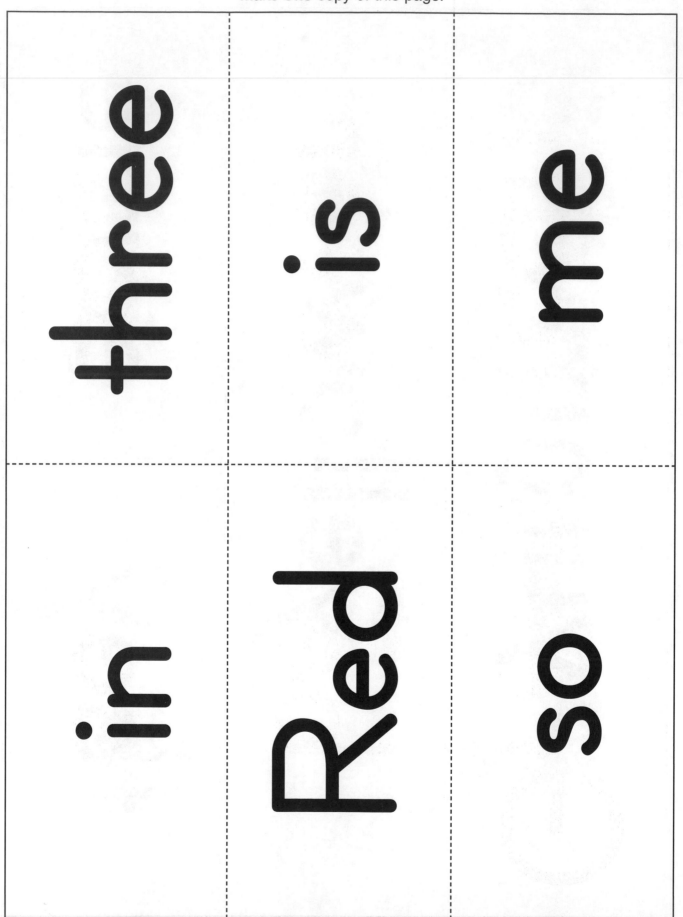

three

is

me

in

Red

so

Make **one** copy of this page.

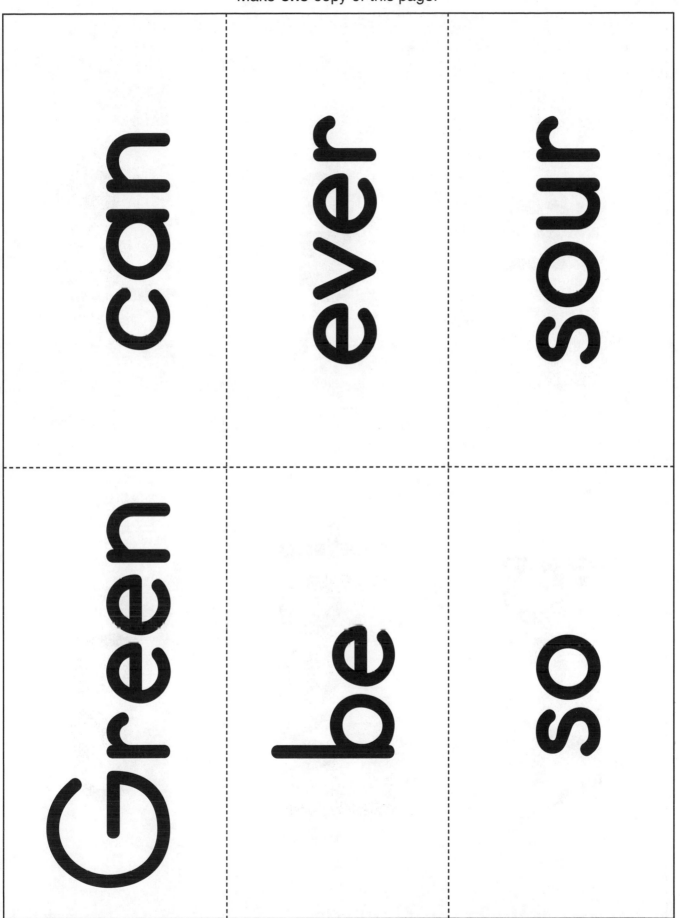

can

ever

sour

Green

be

so

Make **one** copy of this page.

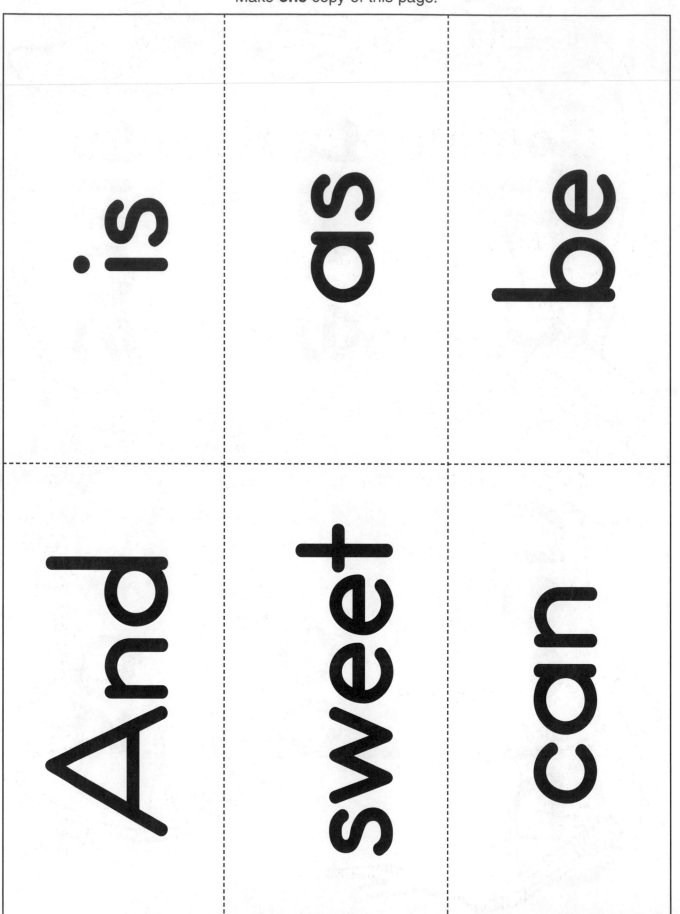

is

as

be

And

sweet

can

Community Helpers

(Sing to the tune of "Are You Sleeping?" or "Frère Jacques")

Community helpers,

Community helpers,

In our town,

In our town,

Teacher and librarian,

Fire fighter, doctor,

Help us learn,

Keep us safe.

Community Helpers

Materials

- age-appropriate fiction and nonfiction books about community helpers
- white board or chart paper and markers
- Community Helpers Song Pocket Chart Cards (pages 70–74) laminated and cut apart
- pocket chart
- markers, colored pencils, and crayons
- Community Helpers Story Writing Page for each child (page 65)
- assembled Community Helpers Mini Book for each student (pages 66–68)
- Fire Fighter Hat Pattern (page 69) and project materials (page 66) for each student

Unit Introduction

1. Read a fictional story about community helpers. Discuss the setting, characters, and plot.

2. Share a nonfiction book about community helpers, pointing out interesting facts.

3. Brainstorm. Write *Community Helpers* at the top of a chart or white board. Ask students to share what they know about community helpers and write down their responses. Use the shared writing technique detailed on page 9.

4. Sing the Community Helpers song while pointing to each of the words on the pocket chart.

5. Pass out the Story Writing Page. Encourage students to write or draw their own stories about community helpers. You can use this time to do some guided writing with small groups or have the children write independently (see page 9).

6. Spend time with each child discussing his or her story or illustration. You will find tips for transcribing and editing students' stories on page 10.

Unit Activities

1. Continue sharing the fiction book about community helpers that you read during the unit introduction. Reread the nonfiction book and discuss interesting facts. Introduce additional books about community helpers during the week.

2. Add student ideas and new facts about community helpers to the brainstorming board.

3. Continue singing the Community Helpers song, pointing to the cards in the pocket chart each time. Remind students that they can use these words in their writing.

4. Use the Community Helpers Mini Book (pages 66–68) for guided or independent writing (see page 9). Encourage students to incorporate new information and ideas they have acquired since beginning the unit.

5. Complete the Fire Fighter Hat Project (pages 66 and 69). Let students wear their hats as they write about community helpers.

My Story About _____

By _____

Community Helpers Mini Book

Materials

- Community Helpers Mini Book patterns (pages 67 and 68)
- gold or yellow construction paper
- white paper
- scissors
- stapler

Assembly Directions

1. Copy pages 67 and 68 (one of each page per student) onto gold or yellow construction paper and cut out the badge shapes to create the front and back covers of the Community Helpers Mini Books.

2. Make copies of the badge pattern (page 68) on white paper and cut them out to make the inside pages of the mini books. For early writers, two pages per book will probably be sufficient. For more experienced writers, increase the number of pages.

3. Assemble the books and staple them together.

Firefighter Hat Project

Materials

- Firefighter Hat Pattern (page 69)
- red construction paper
- tape or stapler
- scissors
- headband strip (heavy paper or tagboard)
- crayons

Preparation

- Make one copy of the Firefighter Hat Pattern (page 69) on red construction paper for each student.

Assembly Directions

1. Have students cut the hat front out.

2. Decorate the front of the firefighter hat.

3. Attach the hat front to the headband.

4. Fit the hatband on students' heads and play fire fighter! Encourage students to write about their experiences.

Community Helpers
Mini Book

Cover

Community Helpers

by _____

Community Helpers
Mini Book *(cont.)*

Back Cover and Inside Pages

Firefighter Hat

Pattern

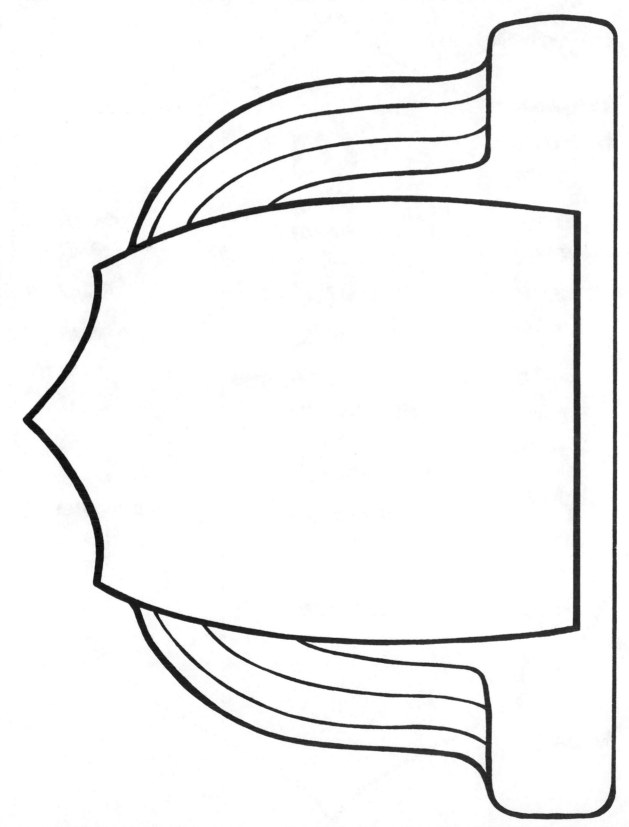

Make **one** copy of this page.

Community

Helpers

doctor

Make **one** copy of this page.

Teacher

librarian

fighter

Make **one** copy of this page.

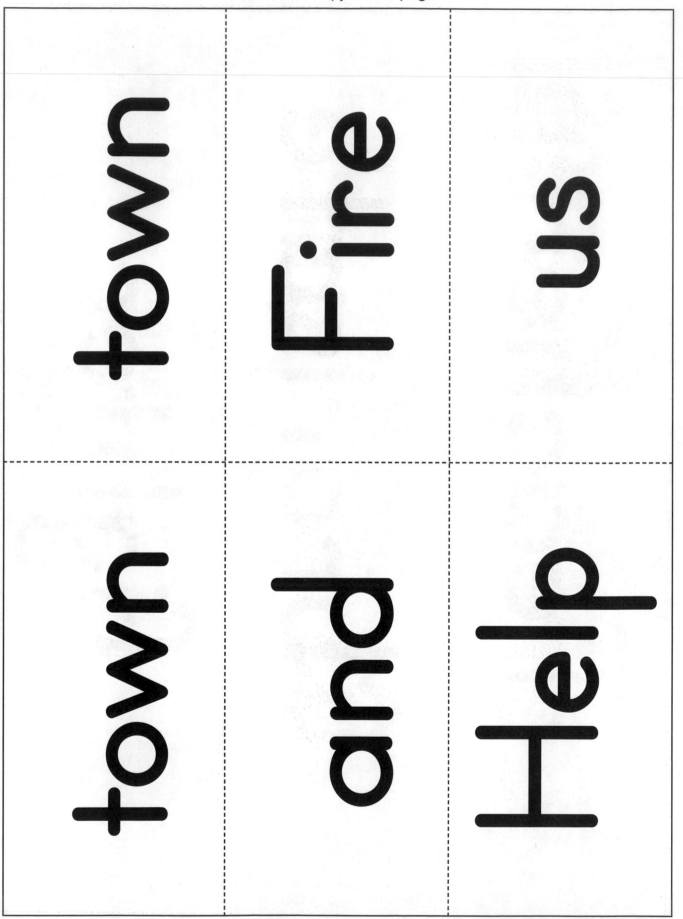

Make **one** copy of this page.

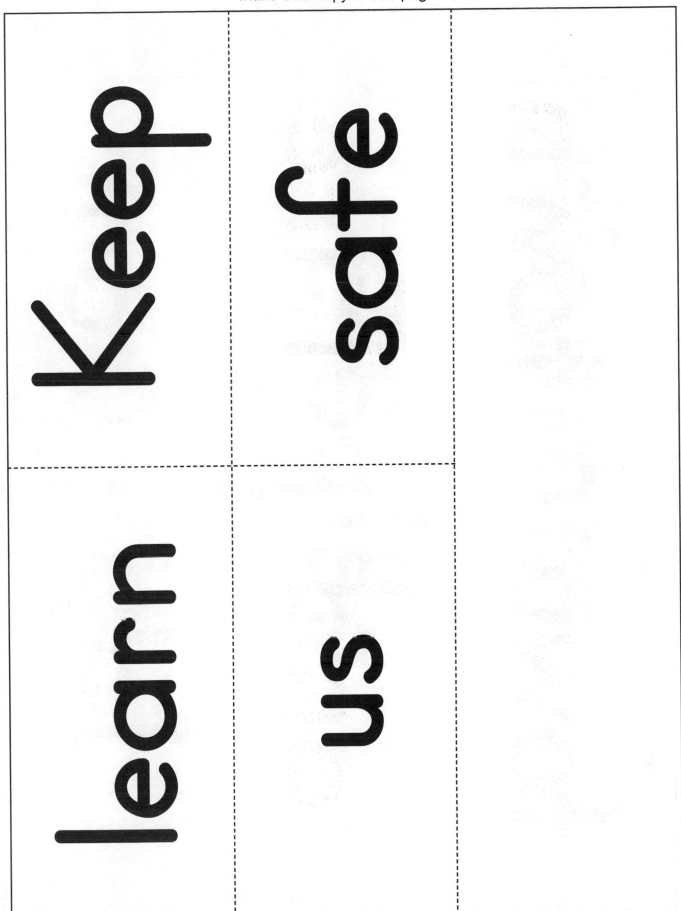

Keep

safe

learn

us

Make **two** copies of this page.

Community

helpers

our

In

The Moon

(Sing to the tune of "Here We Go 'Round the Mulberry Bush")

We will fly high up to the moon,

To the moon,

To the moon,

We will fly high up to the moon,

On a rocket.

The Moon

Materials

- age-appropriate fiction and nonfiction books about the moon
- white board or chart paper and markers
- Moon Song Pocket Chart Cards (pages 82–84) laminated and cut apart
- pocket chart
- markers, colored pencils, and crayons
- Moon Story Writing Page for each child (page 77)
- assembled Moon Mini Book for each student (pages 78–80)
- Rocket Pattern (page 81) and project materials (page 78) for each student

Unit Introduction

1. Read a fictional story about the moon. Discuss the setting, characters, and plot.

2. Share a nonfiction book about the moon, pointing out interesting facts.

3. Brainstorm. Write *The Moon* at the top of a chart or white board. Ask students to share what they know about the moon and write down their responses. Use the shared writing technique detailed on page 9.

4. Sing the Moon song while pointing to each of the words on the pocket chart.

5. Pass out the Story Writing Page. Encourage students to write or draw their own stories about the moon. You can use this time to do some guided writing with small groups or have the children write independently (see page 9).

6. Spend time with each child discussing his or her story or illustration. You will find tips for transcribing and editing students' stories on page 10.

Unit Activities

1. Continue sharing the fiction book about the moon that you read during the unit introduction. Reread the nonfiction book and discuss interesting facts. Introduce additional books about the moon during the week.

2. Add student ideas and new facts about the moon to the brainstorming board.

3. Continue singing the Moon song, pointing to the cards in the pocket chart each time. Remind students that they can use these words in their writing.

4. Use the Moon Mini Book (pages 78–80) for guided or independent writing (see page 9). Encourage students to incorporate new information and ideas they have acquired since beginning the unit.

5. Complete the Rocket Art Project (pages 78 and 81) and let students play with their rockets. Encourage students to write about their experiences.

My Story About _____

By _____

Moon Mini Book

Materials

- Moon Mini Book patterns (pages 79 and 80)
- yellow construction paper
- white paper
- scissors
- stapler

Assembly Directions

1. Copy pages 79 and 80 (one of each page per student) onto yellow construction paper and cut out the moon shapes to create the front and back covers of the Moon Mini Books.

2. Make copies of the moon pattern (page 80) on white paper and cut them out to make the inside pages of the mini books. For early writers, two pages per book will probably be sufficient. For more experienced writers, increase the number of pages.

3. Assemble the books and staple them together.

Rocket Art Project

Materials

- toilet paper tubes
- crayons
- scissors
- glue
- Rocket Pattern (page 81)

Preparation

- Make one copy of the Rocket Pattern (page 81) for each student.

Assembly Directions

1. Give each student a copy of the Rocket Pattern and a toilet paper tube.

2. Have students color and cut out their rockets.

3. Show students how to glue their rockets onto their toilet paper tubes, positioning the rockets so that the bottoms of the rockets are level with the bottoms of the tubes.

4. Let students play astronaut and fly to the moon! Encourage them to write about their experiences.

Moon Mini Book

Cover

The Moon

by _____

Moon Mini Book *(cont.)*

Back Cover and Inside Pages

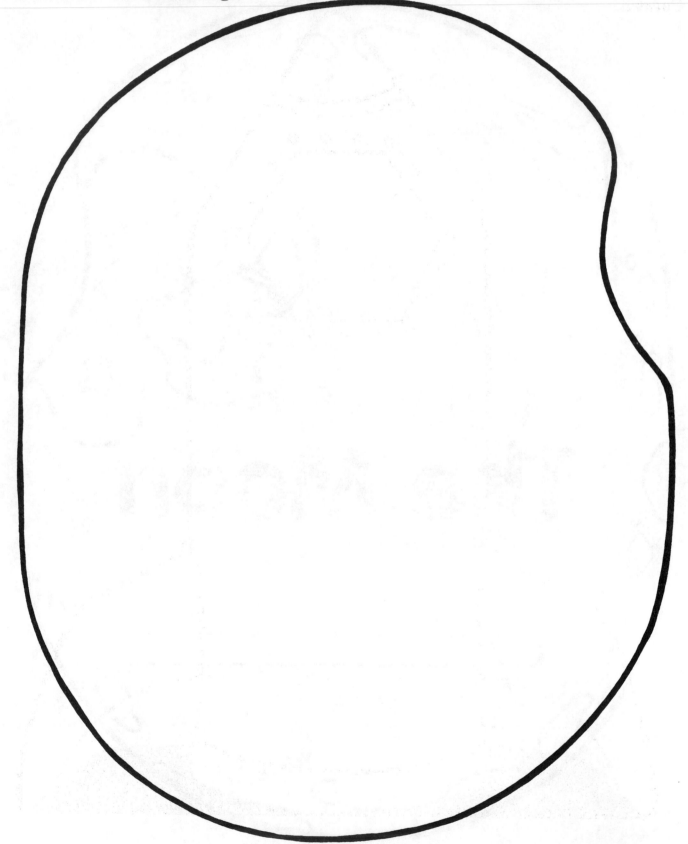

Rocket

Pattern

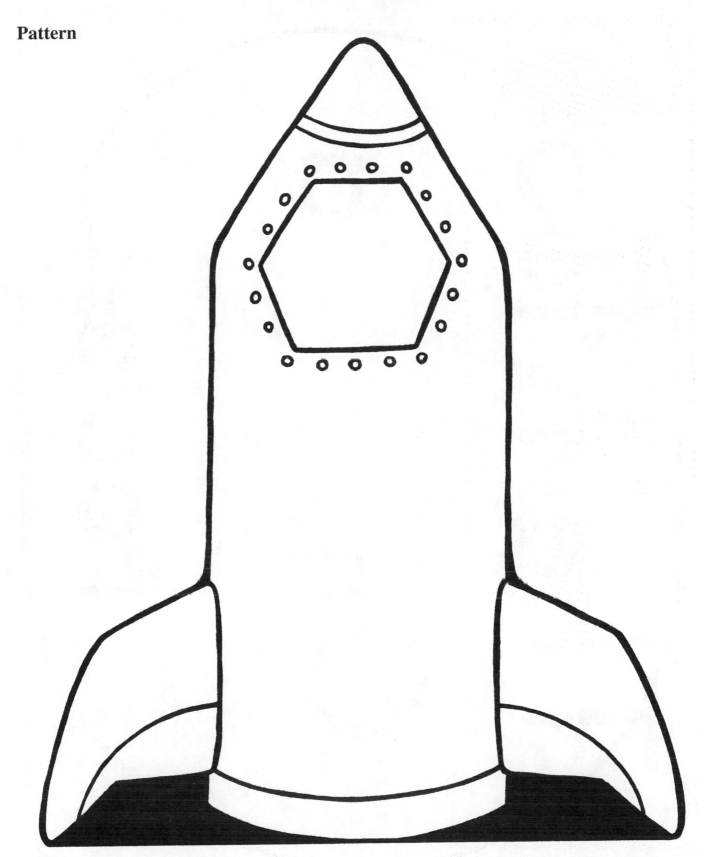

Make **one** copy of this page.

Make **two** copies of this page.

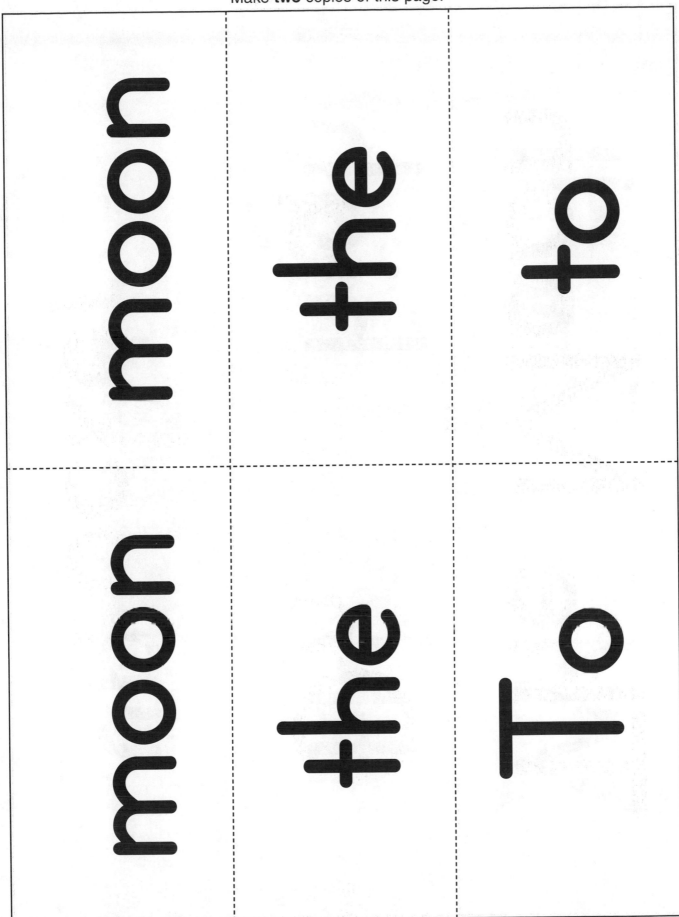

Make **two** copies of this page.

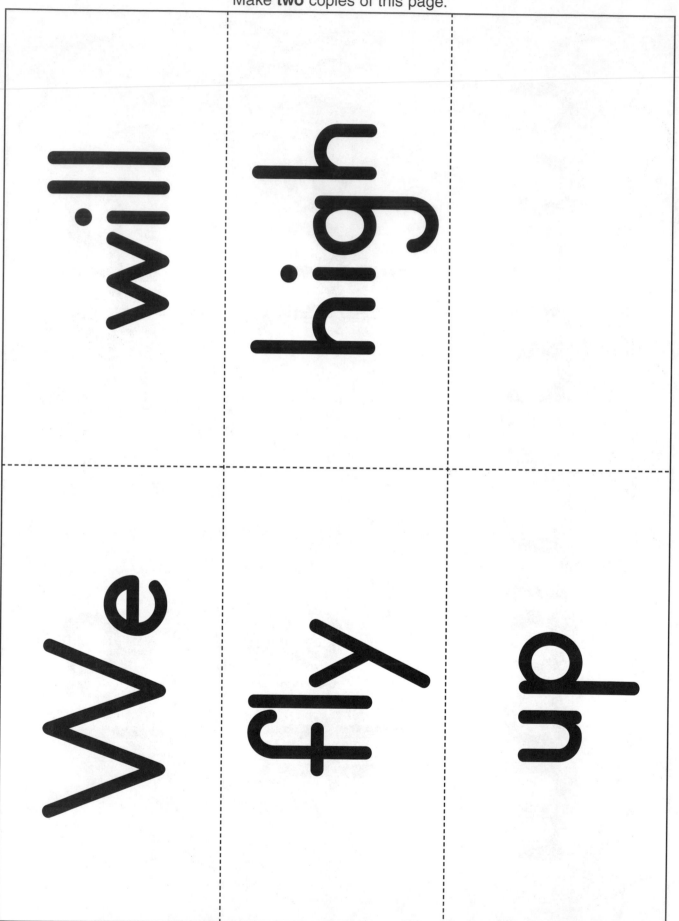

Winter

(Sing to the tune of "London Bridges")

Winter can be so much fun,

In the snow I like to run;

Sledding, snowballs, mittens, hats,

I love winter.

Winter

Winter

snow

fun

Materials

- age-appropriate fiction and nonfiction books about winter
- white board or chart paper and markers
- Winter Song Pocket Chart Cards (pages 92–96) laminated and cut apart
- pocket chart
- markers, colored pencils, and crayons
- Winter Story Writing Page for each child (page 87)
- assembled Winter Mini Book for each student (pages 88–90)
- Snowman Pattern (page 91) and project materials (page 88) for each student

Unit Introduction

1. Read a fictional story about winter. Discuss the setting, characters, and plot.

2. Share a nonfiction book about winter, pointing out interesting facts.

3. Brainstorm. Write *Winter* at the top of a chart or white board. Ask students to share what they know about winter time and write down their responses. Use the shared writing technique detailed on page 9.

4. Sing the Winter song while pointing to each of the words on the pocket chart.

5. Pass out the Story Writing Page. Encourage students to write or draw their own stories about winter. You can use this time to do some guided writing with small groups or have the children write independently (see page 9).

6. Spend time with each child discussing his or her story or illustration. You will find tips for transcribing and editing students' stories on page 10.

Unit Activities

1. Continue sharing the fiction book about winter that you read during the unit introduction. Reread the nonfiction book and discuss interesting facts. Introduce additional books about winter during the week.

2. Add student ideas and new facts about winter to the brainstorming board.

3. Continue singing the Winter song, pointing to the cards in the pocket chart each time. Remind students that they can use these words in their writing.

4. Use the Winter Mini Book (pages 88–90) for guided or independent writing (see page 9). Encourage students to incorporate new information and ideas they have acquired since beginning the unit.

5. Complete the Snowman Art Project (pages 88 and 91), display them in the classroom, and encourage students to write about their work.

My Story About _____

By _____

Winter Mini Book

Materials

- Winter Mini Book patterns (pages 89 and 90)
- white construction paper
- white paper
- scissors
- stapler

Assembly Directions

1. Copy pages 89 and 90 (one of each page per student) onto white construction paper and cut out the snowman shapes to create the front and back covers of the Winter Mini Books.

2. Make copies of the snowman pattern (page 90) on white paper and cut them out to make the inside pages of the mini books. For early writers, two pages per book will probably be sufficient. For more experienced writers, increase the number of pages.

3. Assemble the books and staple them together.

Snowman Art Project

Materials

- Snowman Pattern (page 91)
- scissors
- glue stick or paste
- crayons or markers
- dark blue or black construction paper (one sheet per student)
- salt
- white glue diluted with water
- paint brushes

Preparation

- Make one copy of the Snowman Pattern for each student.

Assembly Directions

1. Show students how to cut out the circles on the Snowman Pattern page and glue them onto the construction paper to make a snowman.

2. Let students add details (eyes, nose, scarf, etc.) to their snowmen with crayons or markers.

3. Help students brush diluted glue all over the construction paper.

4. Let students sprinkle some salt onto the glue. When it dries it will look like the snowmen are in a snowstorm!

5. Display the snowmen in the classroom and encourage students to write captions for or stories about them.

Winter Mini Book

Cover

Winter

by _____

Winter Mini Book *(cont.)*

**Back Cover and
Inside Pages**

Snowman

Pattern

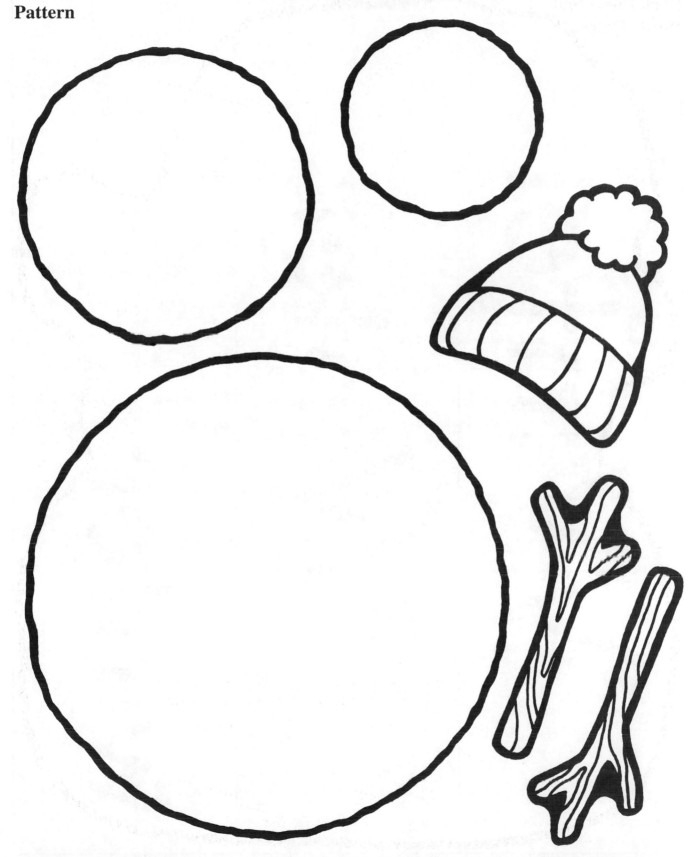

Make **one** copy of this page.

Make **one** copy of this page.

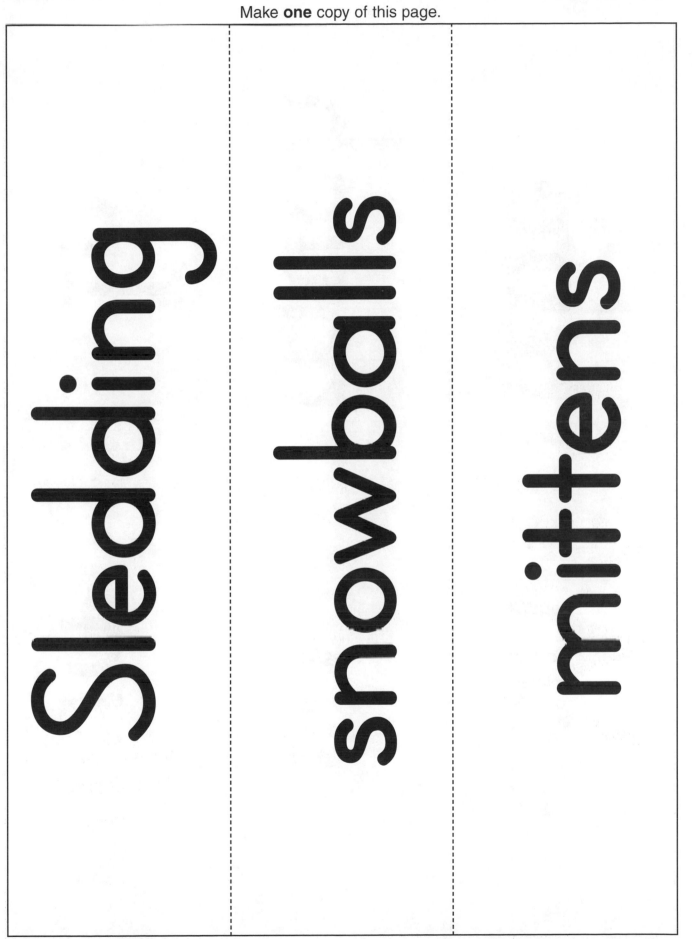

Sledding

snowballs

mittens

Make **one** copy of this page.

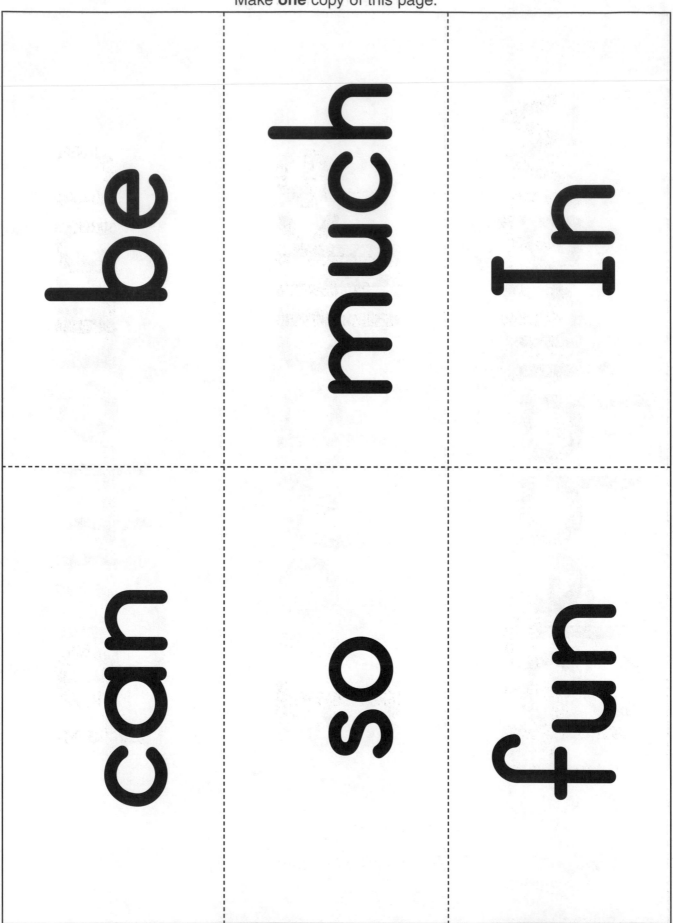

be

much

In

can

so

fun

Make **one** copy of this page.

snow	like	run
the	I	to

Make **one** copy of this page.

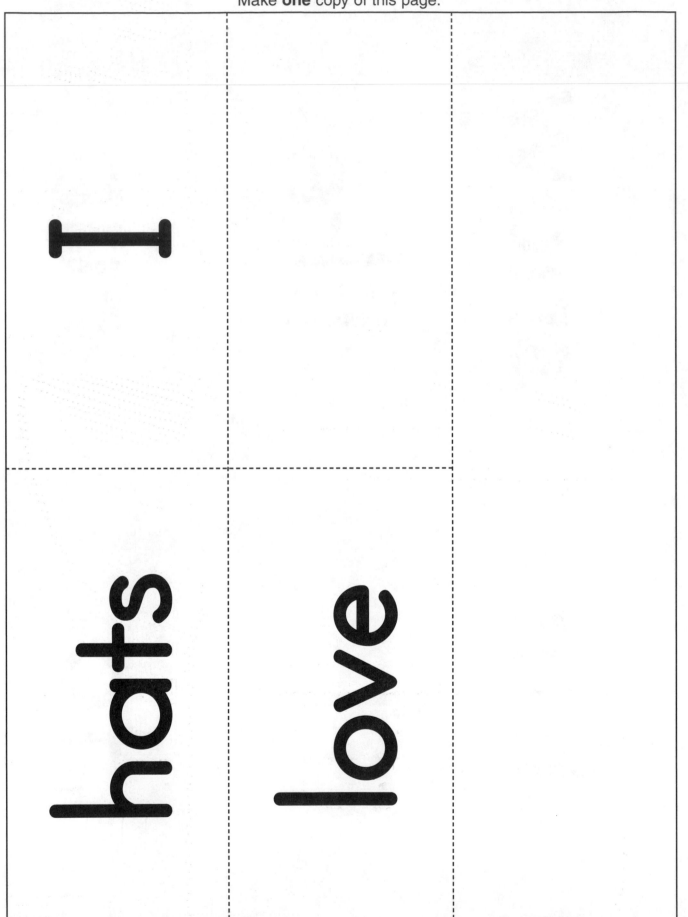

Friends

(Sing to the tune of "Farmer in the Dell")

It's nice to have a friend,

It's nice to have a friend,

We share and care and play all day,

It's nice to have a friend.

It's fun to have a friend,

It's fun to have a friend,

We laugh and love and play all day,

It's fun to have a friend.

Friends

Materials

- age-appropriate fiction and nonfiction books about friends
- white board or chart paper and markers
- Friends Song Pocket Chart Cards (pages 103–106) laminated and cut apart
- pocket chart
- markers, colored pencils, and crayons
- Friends Story Writing Page for each child (page 99)
- assembled Friends Mini Book for each student (pages 100–102)
- Materials for Friendship Necklace Craft (page 100)

Unit Introduction

1. Read a fictional story about friends. Discuss the setting, characters, and plot.

2. Share a nonfiction book about friends, pointing out interesting facts.

3. Brainstorm. Write *Friends* at the top of a chart or white board. Ask students to share what they know about friends and write down their responses. Use the shared writing technique detailed on page 9.

4. Sing the Friends song while pointing to each of the words on the pocket chart.

5. Pass out the Story Writing Page. Encourage students to write or draw their own stories about friends. You can use this time to do some guided writing with small groups or have the children write independently (see page 9).

6. Spend time with each child discussing his or her story or illustration. You will find tips for transcribing and editing students' stories on page 10.

Unit Activities

1. Continue sharing the fiction book about friends that you read during the unit introduction. Reread the nonfiction book and discuss interesting facts. Introduce additional books about friends during the week.

2. Add student ideas and new facts about friends to the brainstorming board.

3. Continue singing the Friends song, pointing to the cards in the pocket chart each time. Remind students that they can use these words in their writing.

4. Use the Friends Mini Book (pages 100–102) for guided or independent writing (see page 9). Encourage students to incorporate new information and ideas they have acquired since beginning the unit.

5. Complete the Friendship Necklace on page 100, share the necklaces, and encourage students to write about their experiences.

My Story About _____

By _____

Friends Mini Book

Materials

- Friends Mini Book patterns (pages 101 and 102)
- colored construction paper
- white paper
- scissors
- stapler

Assembly Directions

1. Copy pages 101 and 102 (one of each page per student) onto colored construction paper and cut out the heart shapes to create the front and back covers of the Friends Mini Books.

2. Make copies of the heart pattern (page 102) on white paper and cut them out to make the inside pages of the mini books. For early writers, two pages per book will probably be sufficient. For more experienced writers, increase the number of pages.

3. Assemble the books and staple them together.

Friendship Necklace

Materials

- colored cereal rings
- piece of yarn or string (one per student)

Preparation

- Tie a cereal ring to the end of each piece of yarn or string.

Assembly Directions

1. Have students wash their hands, then sit in a circle.

2. Show students how to string the colored cereal rings on the yarn.

3. Each student puts a cereal ring on a piece of yarn and then passes it to the next student, who adds a ring. Keep passing the yarn around so that everyone contributes to each necklace.

4. When each piece of yarn is filled with the cereal, tie the ends together to form a necklace.

5. Wear your friendship necklaces and sing the Friends song!

6. Encourage students to write about making and sharing their necklaces. They could write thank you notes to their friends for sharing or write directions for making a friendship necklace.

Friends Mini Book

Cover

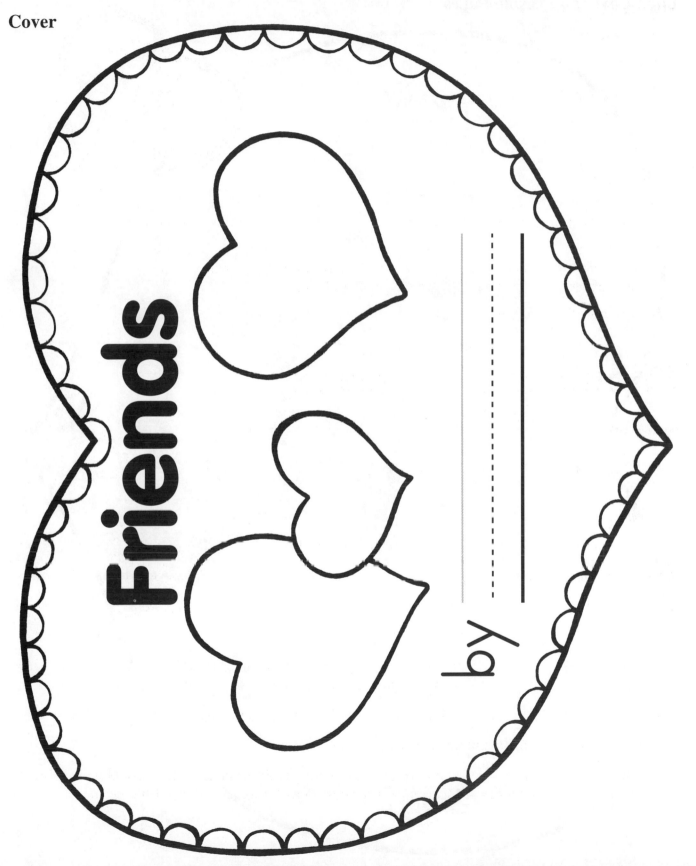

Friends Mini Book *(cont.)*

Back Cover and Inside Pages

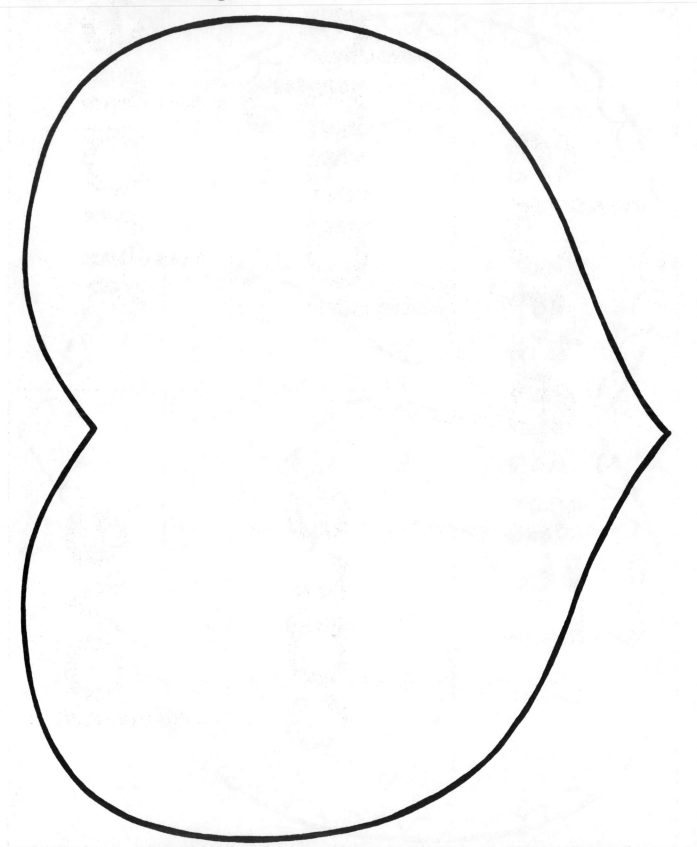

Make **one** copy of this page.

Friends

laugh

share

care

love

Make **three** copies of this page.

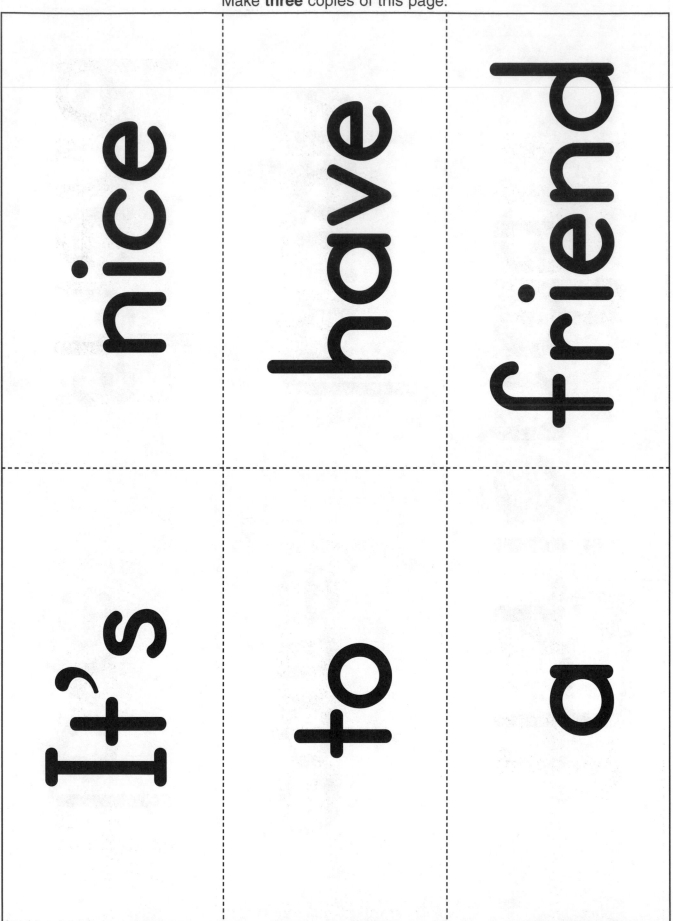

nice

have

friend

It's

to

a

Make **three** copies of this page.

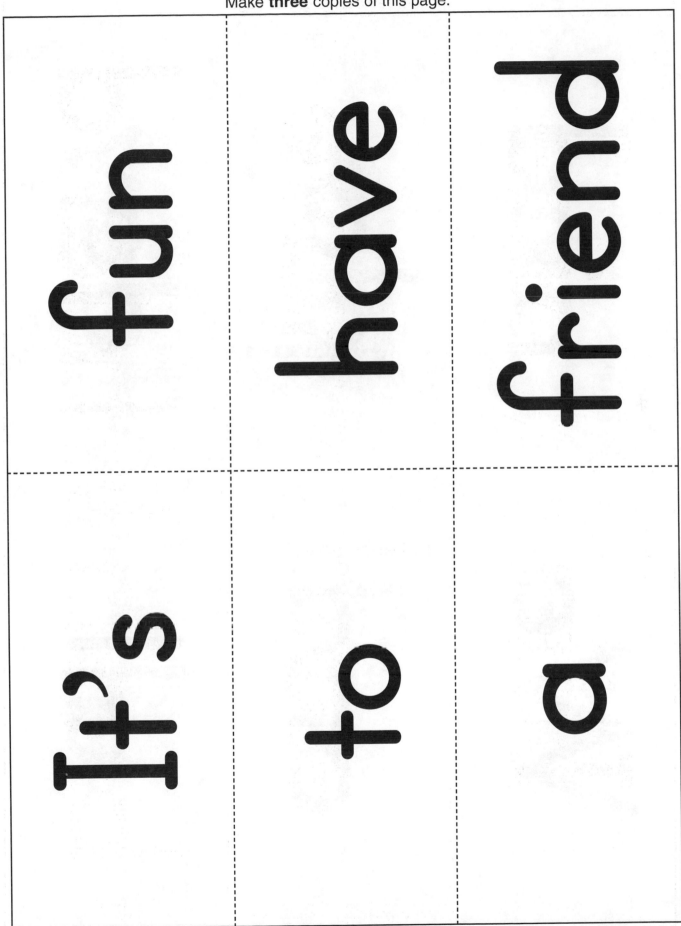

fun

have

friend

It's

to

a

Make **two** copies of this page.

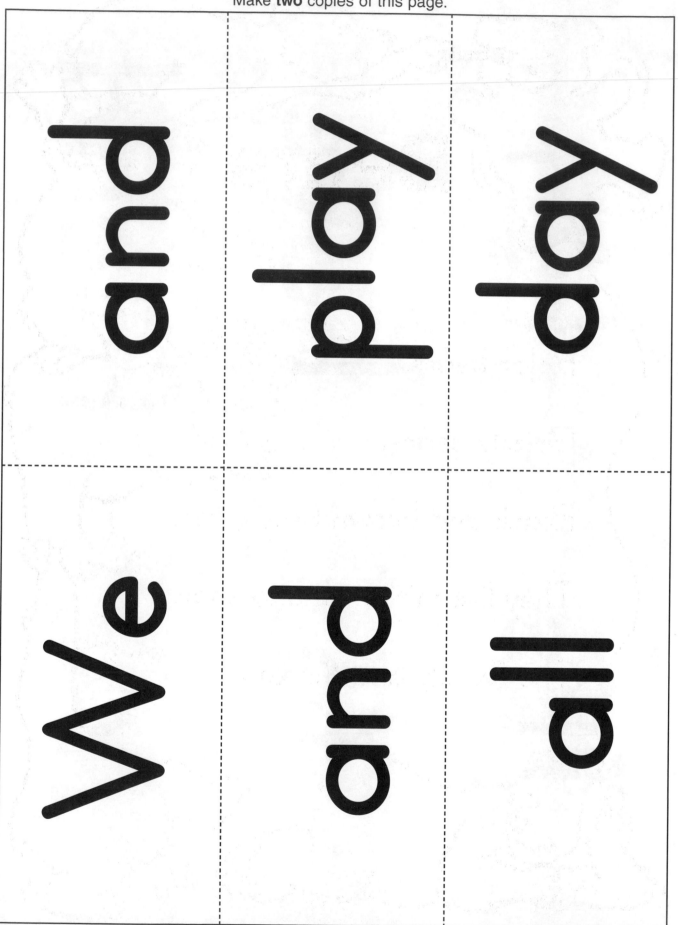

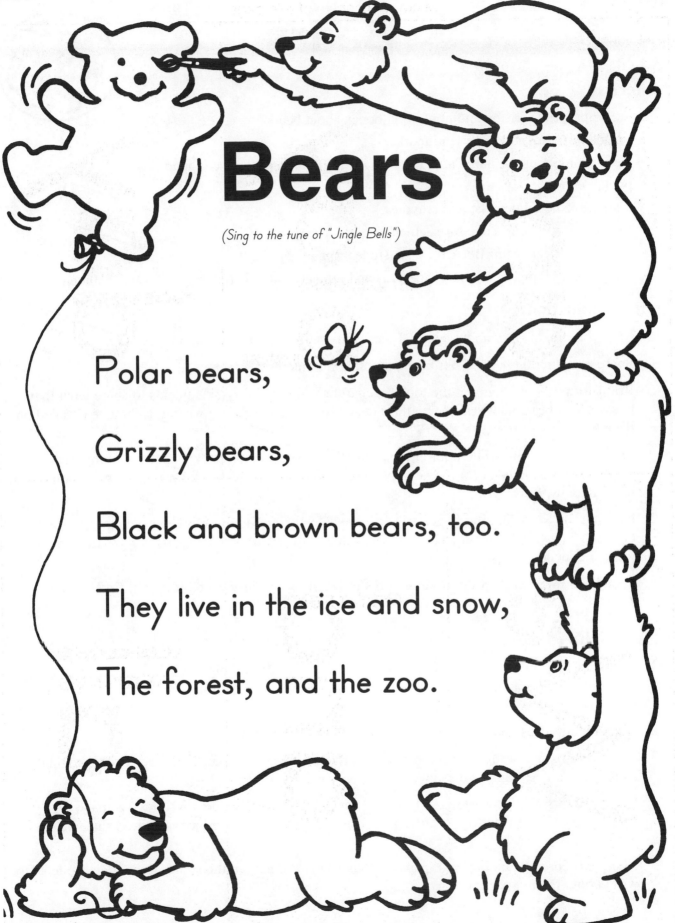

Bears

(Sing to the tune of "Jingle Bells")

Polar bears,

Grizzly bears,

Black and brown bears, too.

They live in the ice and snow,

The forest, and the zoo.

Bears

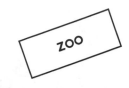

Materials

- age-appropriate fiction and nonfiction books about bears
- white board or chart paper and markers
- Bears Song Pocket Chart Cards (pages 114–118) laminated and cut apart
- pocket chart
- markers, colored pencils, and crayons
- Bears Story Writing Page for each child (page 109)
- assembled Bears Mini Book for each student (pages 110–112)
- Three Bears Puppet Patterns (page 113) and project materials (page 110) for each student

Unit Introduction

1. Read a fictional story about bears. Discuss the setting, characters, and plot.

2. Share a nonfiction book about bears, pointing out interesting facts.

3. Brainstorm. Write *Bears* at the top of a chart or white board. Ask students to share what they know about bears and write down their responses. Use the shared writing technique detailed on page 9.

4. Sing the Bears song while pointing to each of the words on the pocket chart. Picture cards (page 118) are included for the key vocabulary words: grizzly, black (or brown) bear, polar bear, ice and snow, forest, zoo.

5. Pass out the Story Writing Page. Encourage students to write or draw their own stories about bears. You can use this time to do some guided writing with small groups or have the children write independently (see page 9).

6. Spend time with each child discussing his or her story or illustration. You will find tips for transcribing and editing students' stories on page 10.

Unit Activities

1. Continue sharing the fiction book about bears that you read during the unit introduction. Reread the nonfiction book and discuss interesting facts. Introduce additional books about bears during the week.

2. Add student ideas and new facts about bears to the brainstorming board.

3. Continue singing the Bears song, pointing to the cards in the pocket chart each time. Remind students that they can use these words in their writing.

4. Use the Bears Mini Book (pages 110–112) for guided or independent writing (see page 9). Encourage students to incorporate new information and ideas they have acquired since beginning the unit.

5. Make the Three Bears Puppets (pages 110 and 113) and act out the story. Encourage students to write about their experiences.

My Story About _____

By _____

Bears Mini Book

Materials

- Bears Mini Book patterns (pages 111 and 112)
- brown construction paper
- white paper
- scissors
- stapler

Assembly Directions

1. Copy pages 111 and 112 (one of each page per student) onto brown construction paper and cut out the bear shapes to create the front and back covers of the Bears Mini Book.

2. Make copies of the bear pattern (page 112) on white paper and cut them out to make the inside pages of the mini books. For early writers, two pages per book will probably be sufficient. For more experienced writers, increase the number of pages.

3. Assemble the books and staple them together.

The Three Bears Puppets

Materials

- The Three Bears Puppet Patterns (page 113)
- crayons
- scissors
- glue or paste
- craft sticks (four per student)

Preparation

- Make one copy of each of the Three Bears Puppets Patterns for each student.

Assembly Directions

1. Let students color the mamma bear, papa bear, baby bear, and Goldilocks puppet patterns.

2. Help students cut out the bears and Goldilocks. Use the dashed lines as guides.

3. Have students glue each puppet onto a craft stick.

4. Let students use the puppets to tell the story of the Three Bears and encourage them to write about their experiences.

Bears Mini Book

Cover

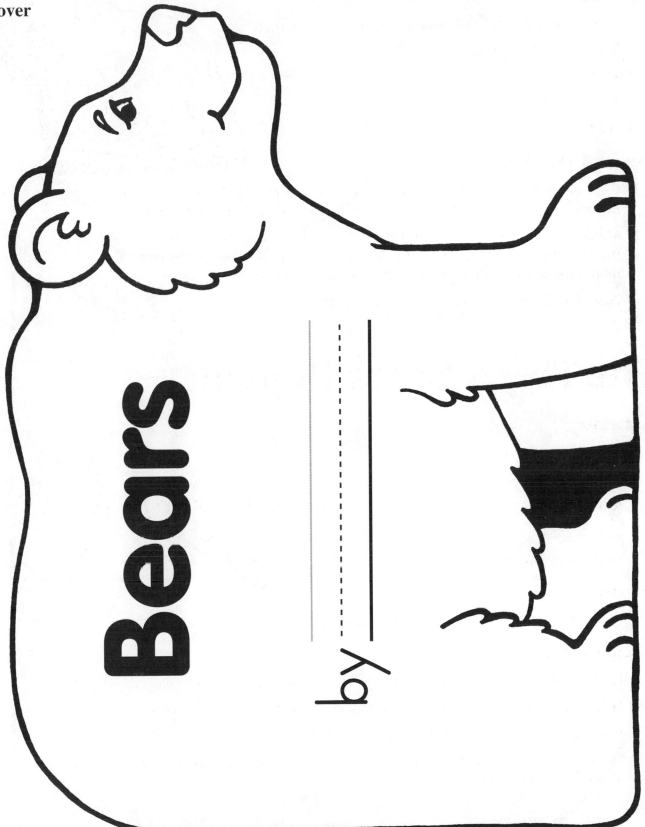

Bears Mini Book *(cont.)*

Back Cover and Inside Pages

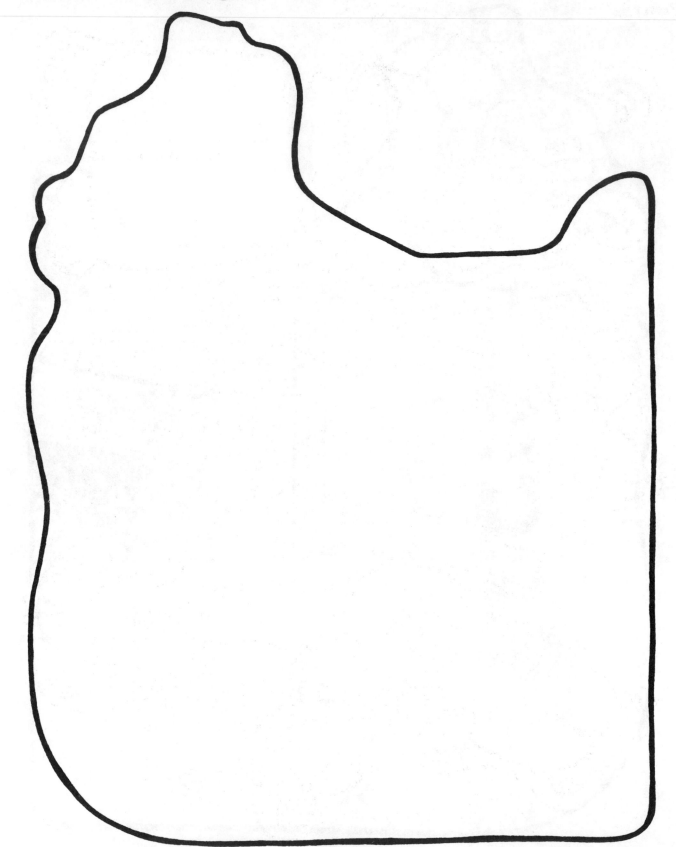

Three Bears Puppets

Patterns

Make **one** copy of this page.

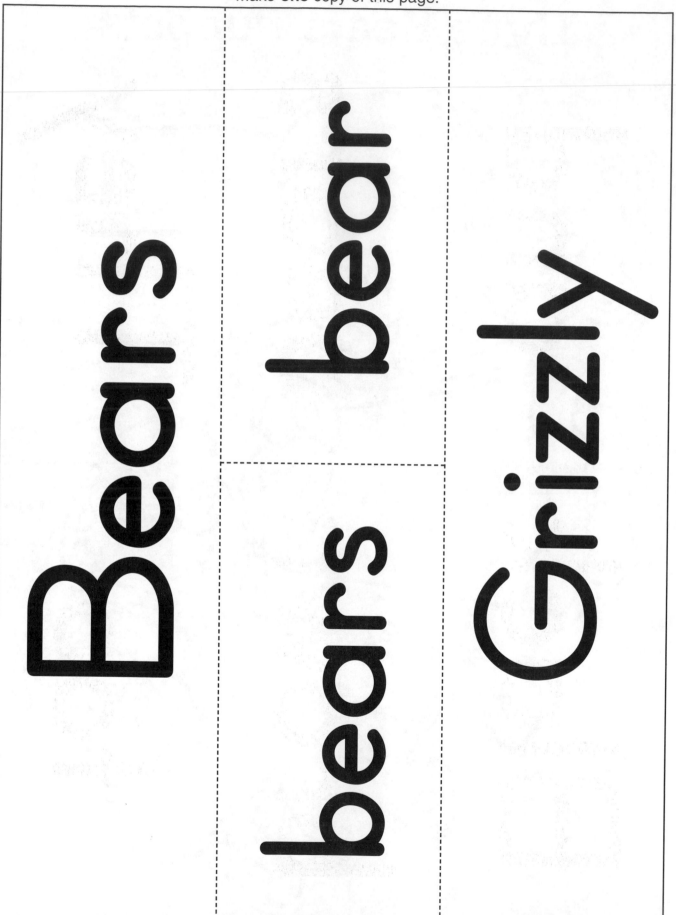

Make **one** copy of this page.

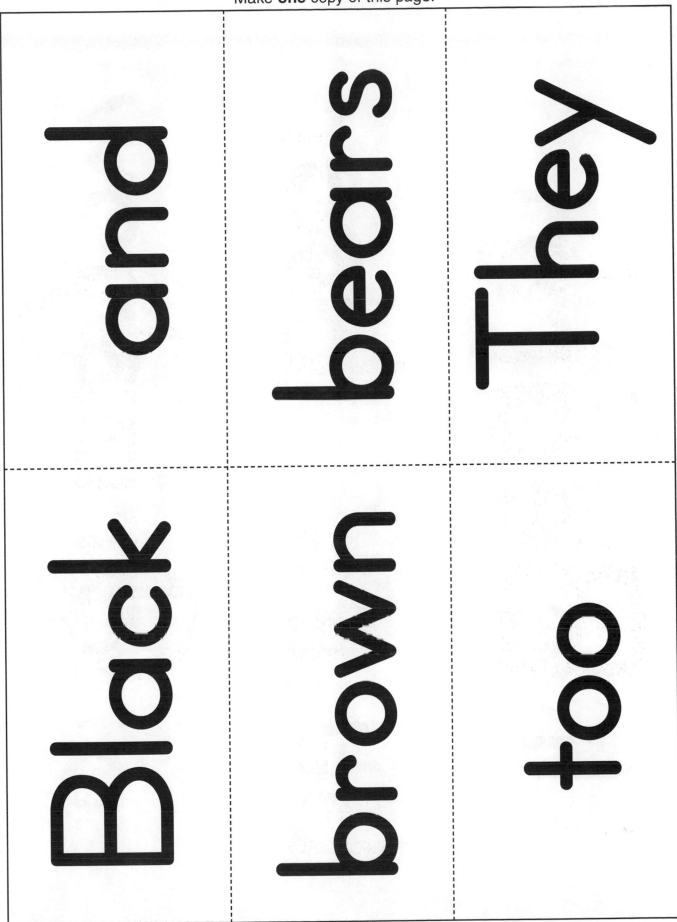

and

bears

They

Black

brown

too

Make **one** copy of this page.

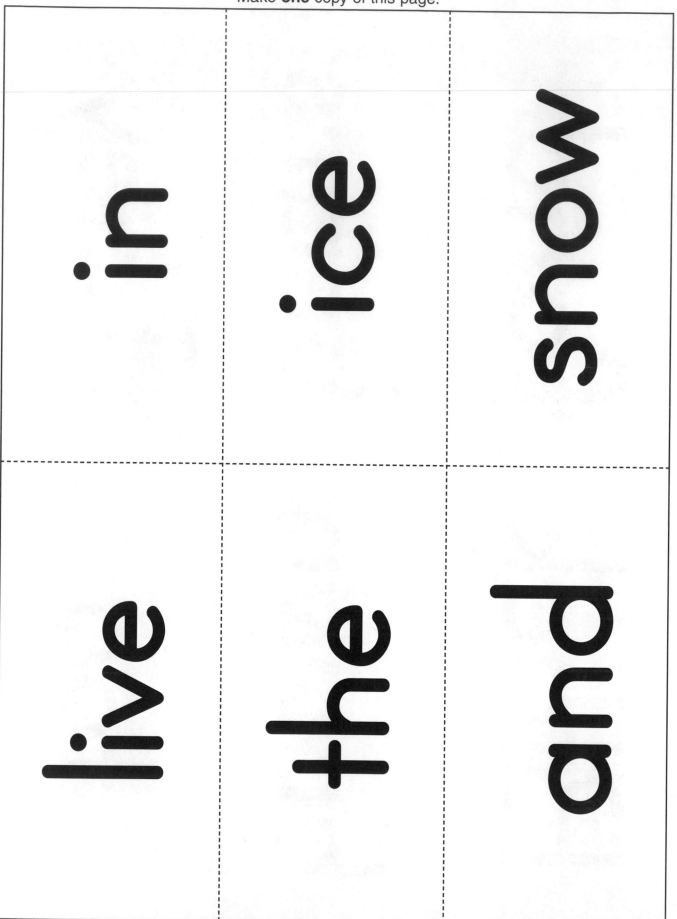

in

ice

snow

live

the

and

Make **one** copy of this page.

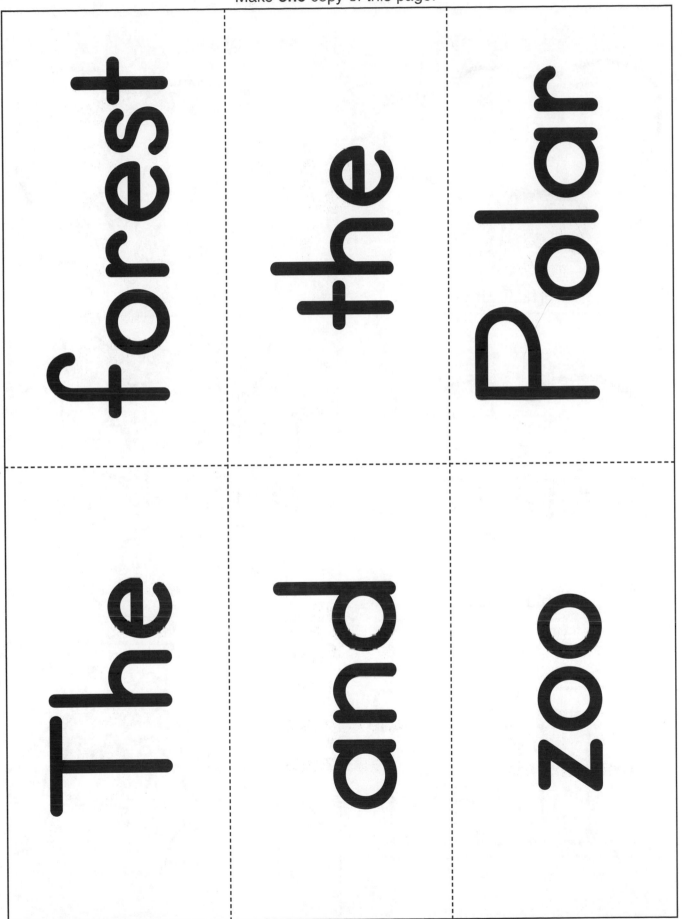

forest

the

Polar

The

and

zoo

Make **one** copy of this page.

grizzly bear

polar bear

black bear

ZOO

Stars

(Sing to the tune of "It's a Small World")

Stars are shining in the sky,

See them twinkle up so high,

Stars are shining in the sky,

In the dark, night sky.

Stars

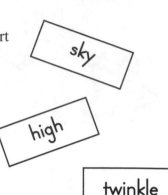

Materials

- age-appropriate fiction and nonfiction books about stars
- white board or chart paper and markers
- Stars Song Pocket Chart Cards (pages 125–128) laminated and cut apart
- pocket chart
- markers, colored pencils, and crayons
- Stars Story Writing Page for each child (page 121)
- assembled Stars Mini Book for each student (pages 122–124)
- materials for Starry Sky Art Project (page 122)

sky

high

twinkle

Unit Introduction

1. Read a fictional story about stars. Discuss the setting, characters, and plot.

2. Share a nonfiction book about stars, pointing out interesting facts.

3. Brainstorm. Write *Stars* at the top of a chart or white board. Ask students to share what they know about stars and write down their responses. Use the shared writing technique detailed on page 9.

4. Sing the Stars song while pointing to each of the words on the pocket chart.

5. Pass out the Stars Story Writing Page. Encourage students to write or draw their own stories about stars. You can use this time to do some guided writing with small groups or have the children write independently (see page 9).

6. Spend time with each child discussing his or her story or illustration. You will find tips for transcribing and editing students' stories on page 10.

Unit Activities

1. Continue sharing the fiction book about stars that you read during the unit introduction. Reread the nonfiction book and discuss interesting facts. Introduce additional books about stars during the week.

2. Add student ideas and new facts about stars to the brainstorming board.

3. Continue singing the Stars song, pointing to the cards in the pocket chart each time. Remind students that they can use these words in their writing.

4. Use the Stars Mini Book (pages 122–124) for guided or independent writing (see page 9). Encourage students to incorporate new information and ideas they have acquired since beginning the unit.

5. Complete the Starry Sky Art Project on page 122, display them in the classroom, and encourage students to write about their work.

My Story About _____

By _____

Stars Mini Book

Materials

- Stars Mini Book patterns (pages 123 and 124)
- yellow construction paper
- white paper
- scissors
- stapler

Assembly Directions

1. Copy pages 123 and 124 (one of each page per student) onto yellow construction paper and cut out the star shapes to create the front and back covers of the Stars Mini Books.

2. Make copies of the star pattern (page 124) on white paper and cut them out to make the inside pages of the mini books. For early writers, two pages per book will probably be sufficient. For more experienced writers, increase the number of pages.

3. Assemble the books and staple them together.

Starry Sky Art Project

Materials

- light colored (pale pink, light blue, pale yellow, etc.) construction paper (one per student)
- white crayons or china markers
- black or dark blue tempra paint
- paint brushes

Preparation

- Make a mixture of one part tempra paint and two parts water.

Directions

1. Show students how to draw stars on the construction paper with a white crayon or china marker. Tell them to draw plenty of stars to fill up the sky. If students have difficulty drawing stars, show them how to make two overlapping X's or large dots.

2. Have students paint the tempera/water mix over their entire papers. The crayon or china marker will resist the paint and the stars will show through to create a night sky.

3. Display the students' starry skies and encourage them to write captions for or stories about their art.

Stars Mini Book

Cover

Stars Mini Book *(cont.)*

Back Cover and Inside Pages

Make **one** copy of this page.

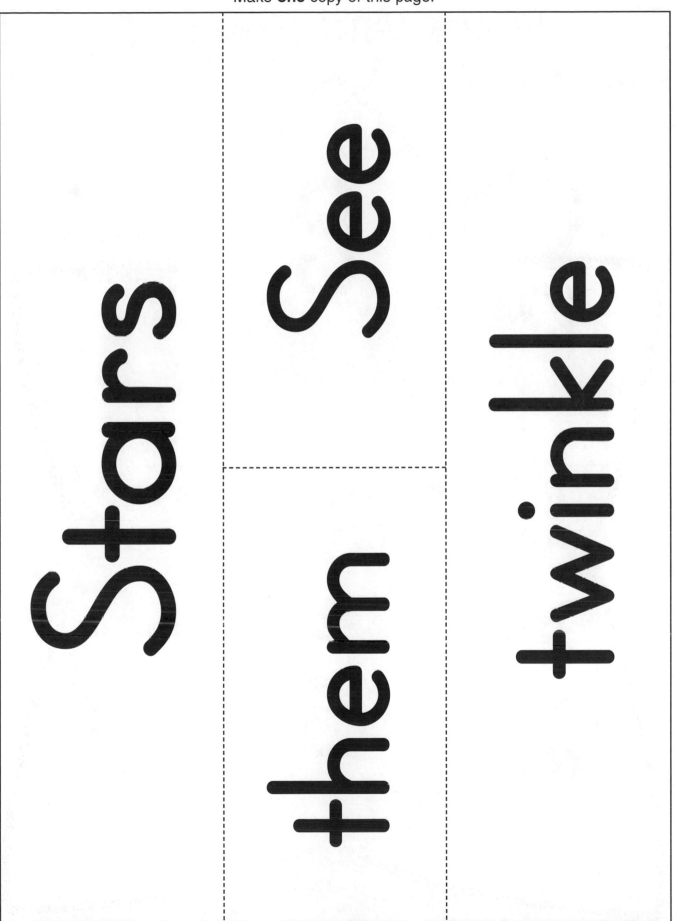

Stars

See

them

twinkle

Make **one** copy of this page.

sky	so	In
sky	up	high

Make **one** copy of this page.

dark

sky

the

night

Make **two** copies of this page.

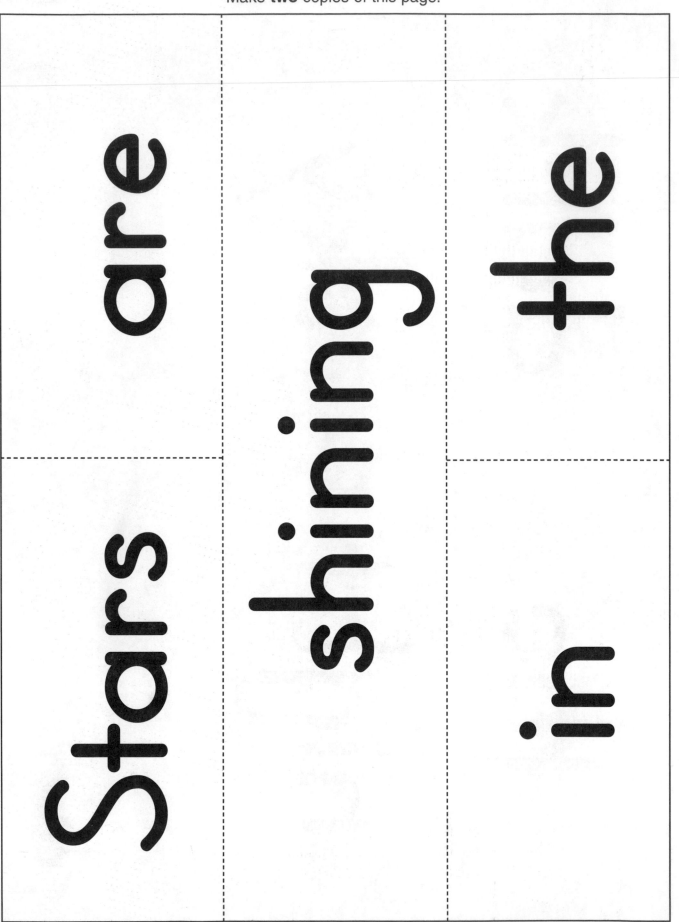

are

shining

the

Stars

in

Spring

(Sing to the tune of "My Darling Clementine")

When it's springtime and it's windy,

Then a kite I like to fly.

When it rains on my umbrella,

See a rainbow in the sky.

Oh it's springtime,

Oh it's springtime,

When the rain makes flowers grow.

Say hello to pretty sunshine,

Say goodbye to melting snow.

Spring

springtime

flowers

umbrellas

Materials

- age-appropriate fiction and nonfiction books about spring
- white board or chart paper and markers
- Spring Song Pocket Chart Cards (pages 136–144) laminated and cut apart
- pocket chart
- markers, colored pencils, and crayons
- Spring Story Writing Page for each child (page 131)
- assembled Spring Mini Book for each student (pages 132–134)
- Rainbow Pattern (page 135) and project materials (page 132) for each student

Unit Introduction

1. Read a fictional story about spring. Discuss the setting, characters, and plot.

2. Share a nonfiction book about spring, pointing out interesting facts.

3. Brainstorm. Write *Spring* at the top of a chart or white board. Ask students to share what they know about springtime and write down their responses. Use the shared writing technique detailed on page 9.

4. Sing the Spring song while pointing to each of the words on the pocket chart. Picture cards (page 144) are included for the key vocabulary words.

5. Pass out the Story Writing Page. Encourage students to write or draw their own stories about spring. You can use this time to do some guided writing with small groups or have the children write independently (see page 9).

6. Spend time with each child discussing his or her story or illustration. You will find tips for transcribing and editing students' stories on page 10.

Unit Activities

1. Continue sharing the fiction book about spring that you read during the unit introduction. Reread the nonfiction book and discuss interesting facts. Introduce additional books about spring during the week.

2. Add student ideas and new facts about spring to the brainstorming board.

3. Continue singing the Spring song, pointing to the cards in the pocket chart each time. Remind students that they can use these words in their writing.

4. Use the Spring Mini Book (pages 132–134) for guided or independent writing (see page 9). Encourage students to incorporate new information and ideas they have acquired since beginning the unit.

5. Complete the Spring Scene Art Project (pages 132 and 135), display them in the classroom, and encourage students to write about their work.

My Story About _____

By _____

Spring Mini Book

Materials

- Spring Mini Book patterns (pages 133 and 134)
- colored construction paper
- white paper
- scissors
- stapler

Assembly Directions

1. Copy pages 133 and 134 (one of each page per student) onto colored construction paper and cut out the kite shapes to create the front and back covers of the Spring Mini Books.

2. Make copies of the kite pattern (page 134) on white paper and cut them out to make the inside pages of the mini books. For early writers, two pages per book will probably be sufficient. For more experienced writers, increase the number of pages.

3. Assemble the books and staple them together.

Spring Scene Art Project

Materials

- Rainbow Pattern (page 135)
- crayons or markers
- cotton balls
- paper cupcake holders
- glue or paste
- large sheets of light blue construction paper (11" x 17")
- scissors

Preparation

- Copy the Rainbow Pattern on white paper (one page per student).

Assembly Directions

1. Give each student a Rainbow Pattern page. Have them color the rainbow and cut it out.

2. Show students how to glue or paste the rainbow across the corner of the construction paper. Let them glue on cotton balls for clouds.

3. Show students how to draw grass and flower stems at the bottom of the construction paper. Have them glue or paste a cupcake holder on top of each stem to make flowers.

4. Students can use crayons or markers to add details to their pictures such as raindrops, kites, people, or animals. Remind them that they can use their brainstorming board for ideas.

5. Display students' spring scenes in the classroom and encourage them to write captions for stories about their art.

Spring Mini Book

Cover

Spring

by _____

Spring Mini Book *(cont.)*

Back Cover and Inside Pages

Rainbow

Pattern

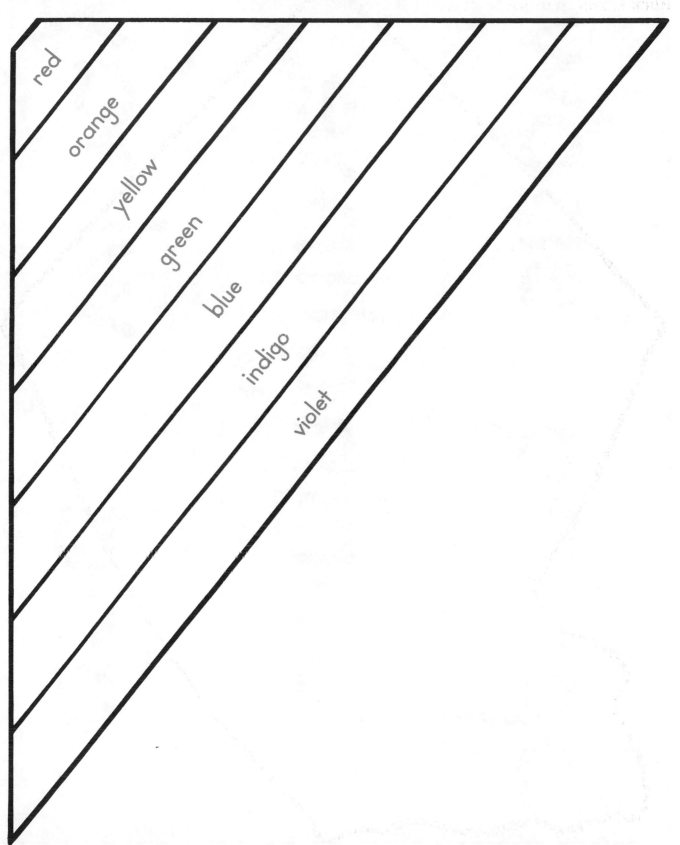

Make **one** copy of this page.

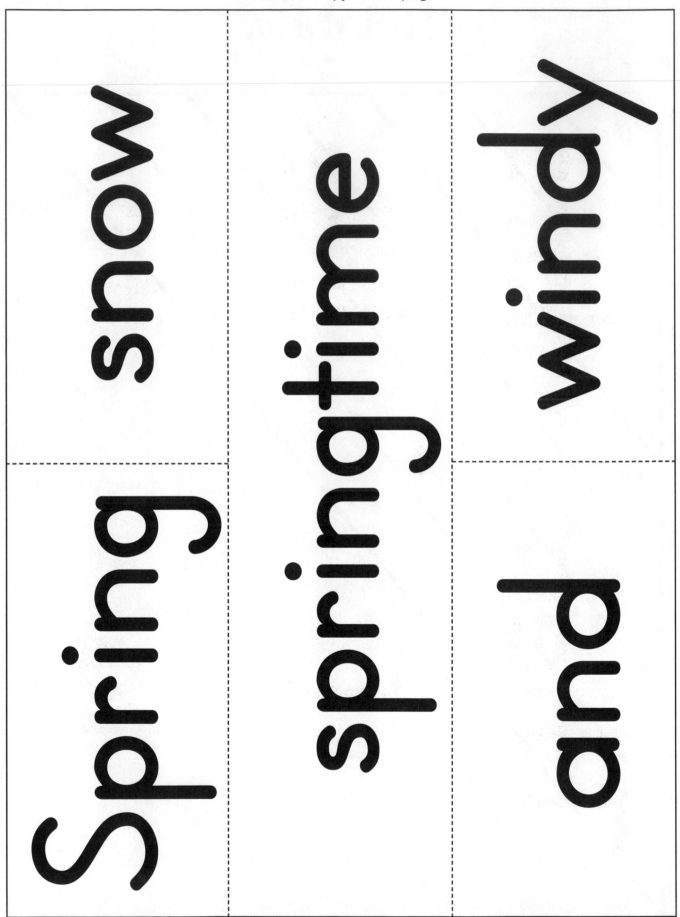

snow

springtime

windy

Spring

spring

and

Make **one** copy of this page.

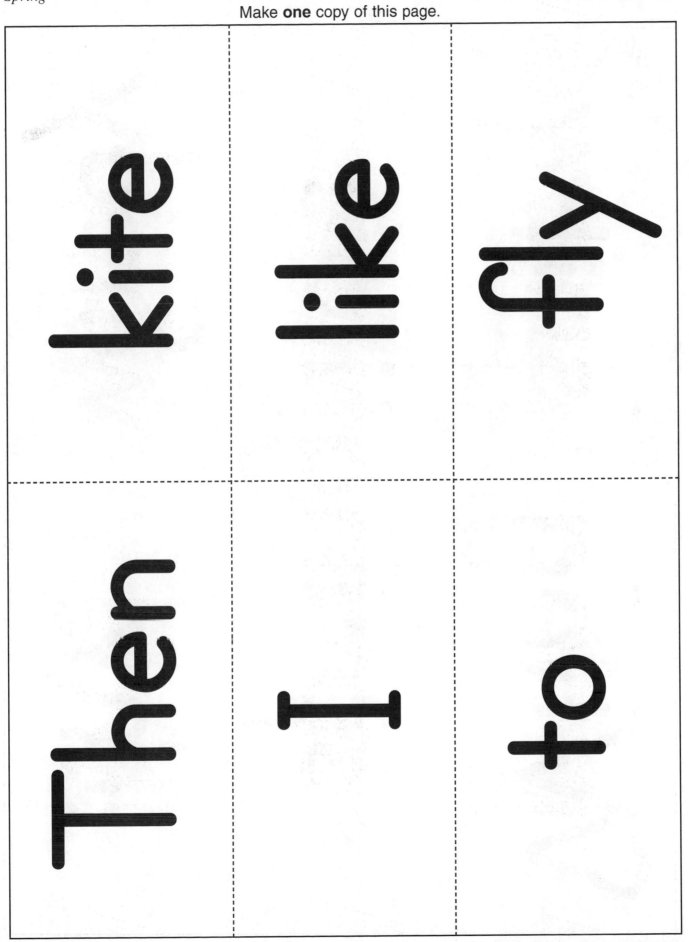

kite

like

fly

Then

I

to

Make **one** copy of this page.

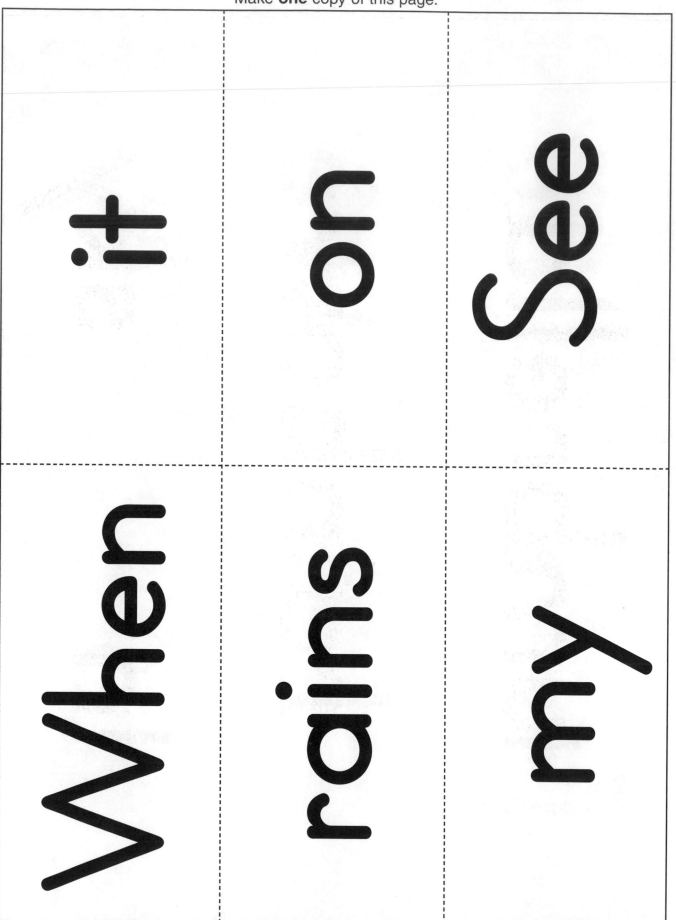

it

on

See

When

rains

my

Make **one** copy of this page.

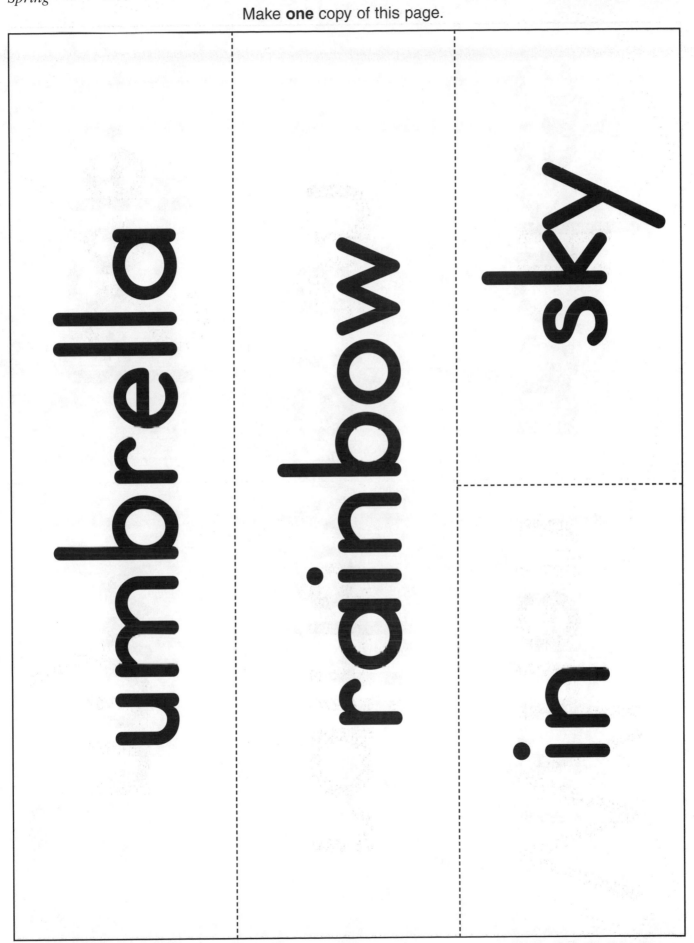

umbrella

rainbow

sky

in

Make **one** copy of this page.

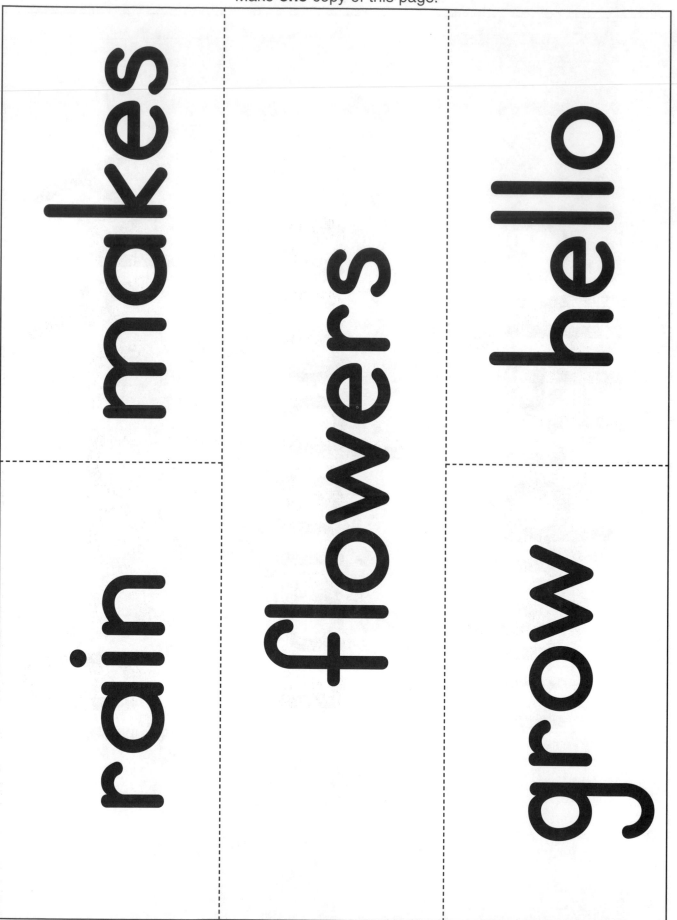

makes

flowers

hello

rain

grow

Make **one** copy of this page.

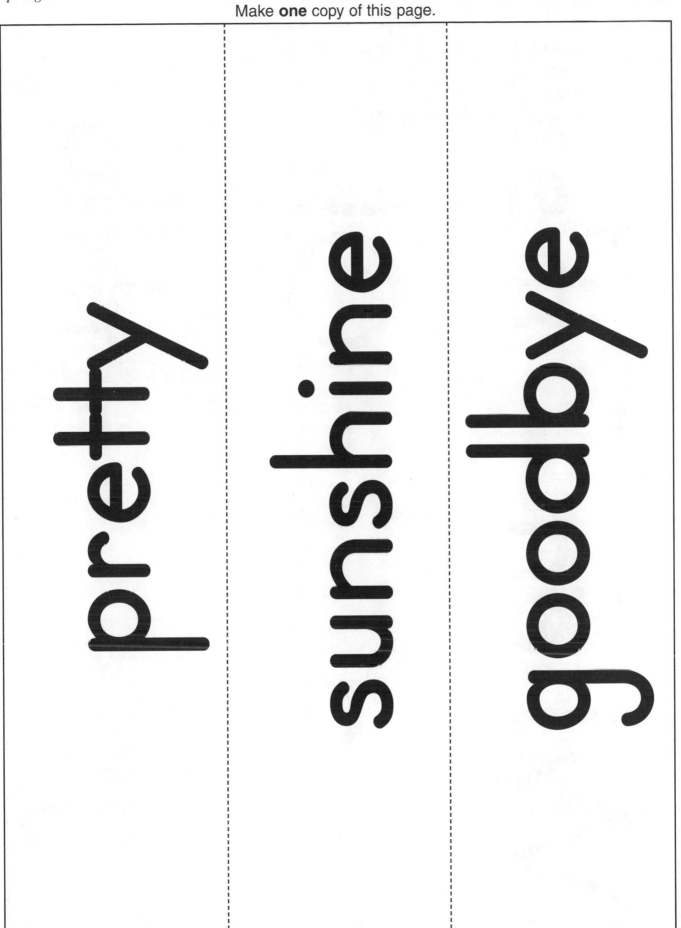

pretty

sunshine

goodbye

Make **two** copies of this page.

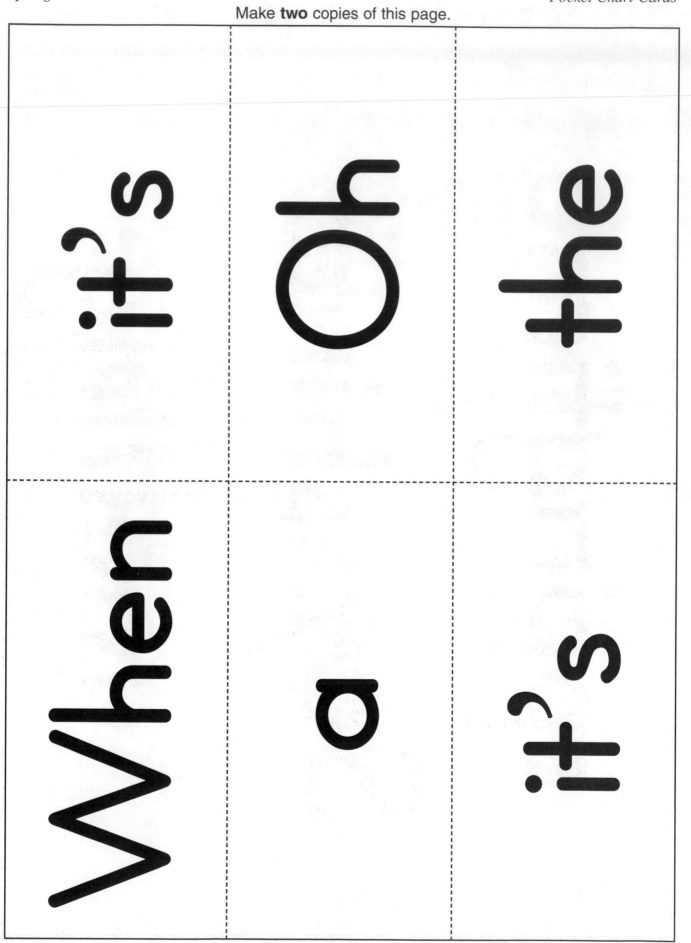

it's

Oh

the

When

a

it's

Make **two** copies of this page. **Note:** "Melting" is only used once.

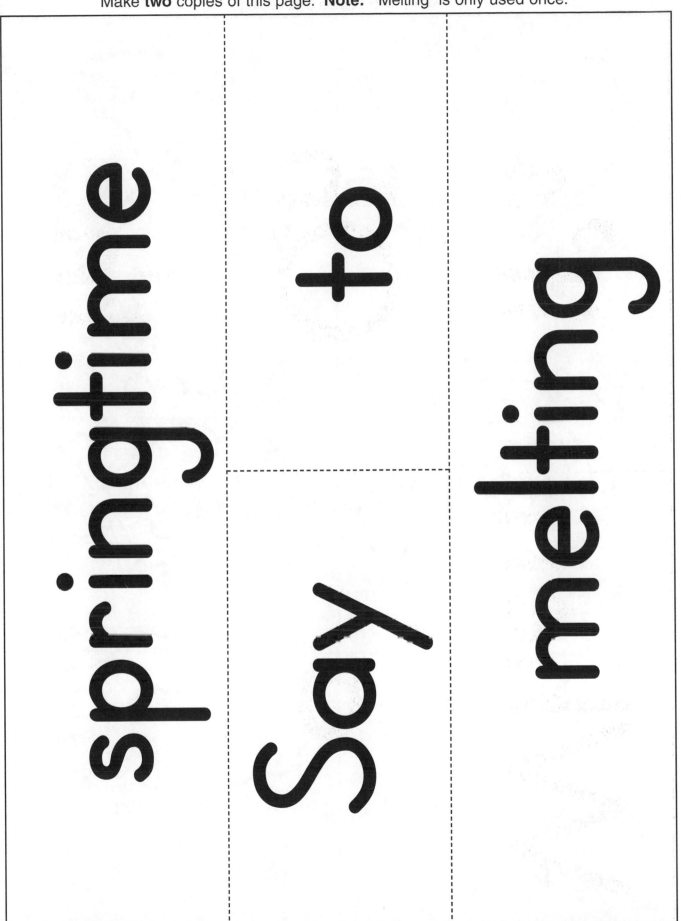

springtime

to

Say

melting

Make **two** copies of this page.

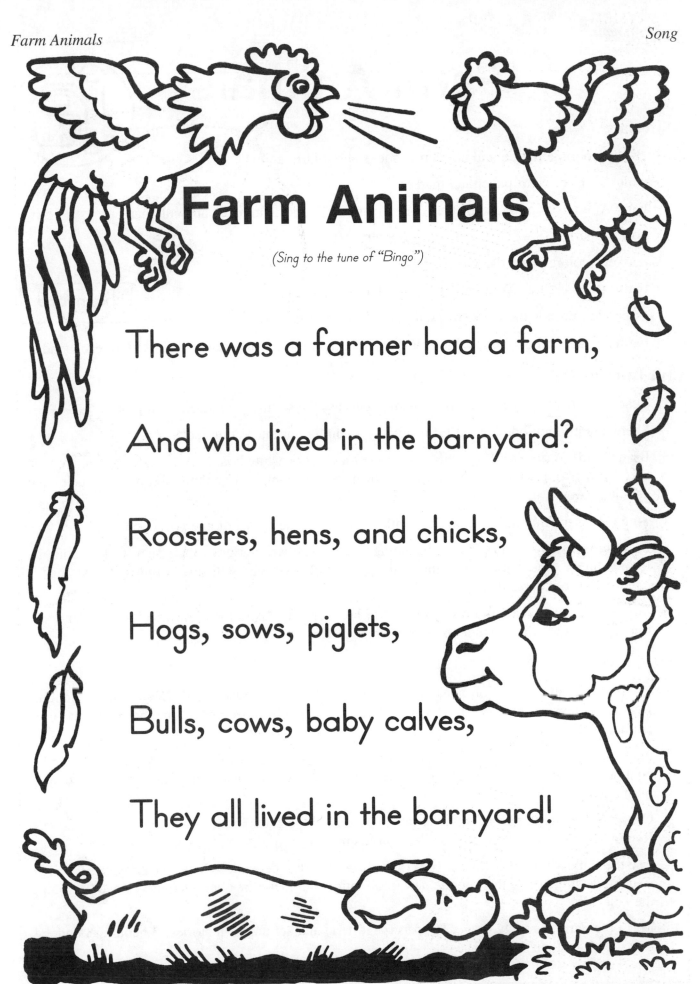

Farm Animals

(Sing to the tune of "Bingo")

There was a farmer had a farm,

And who lived in the barnyard?

Roosters, hens, and chicks,

Hogs, sows, piglets,

Bulls, cows, baby calves,

They all lived in the barnyard!

#3224 Emergent Writer's Workshop

Farm Animals

Materials

- age-appropriate fiction and nonfiction books about farm animals
- white board or chart paper and markers
- Farm Animals Song Pocket Chart Cards (pages 152–156) laminated and cut apart
- pocket chart
- markers, colored pencils, and crayons
- Farm Animals Story Writing Page for each child (page 147)
- assembled Barn Mini Book for each student (pages 148–150)
- Farm Animals Finger Puppet Patterns (page 151) and project materials (page 148) for each student

farm

barnyard

Unit Introduction

1. Read a fictional story about farm animals. Discuss the setting, characters, and plot.

2. Share a nonfiction book about farm animals, pointing out interesting facts.

3. Brainstorm. Write *Farm Animals* at the top of a chart or white board. Ask students to share what they know about farm animals and write down their responses. Use the shared writing technique detailed on page 9.

4. Sing the Farm Animals song while pointing to each of the words on the pocket chart.

5. Pass out the Story Writing Page. Encourage students to write or draw their own stories about farm animals. You can use this time to do some guided writing with small groups or have the children write independently (see page 9).

6. Spend time with each child discussing his or her story or illustration. You will find tips for transcribing and editing students' stories on page 10.

Unit Activities

1. Continue sharing the fiction book about farm animals that you read during the unit introduction. Reread the nonfiction book and discuss interesting facts. Introduce additional books about farm animals during the week.

2. Add student ideas and new facts about farm animals to the brainstorming board. Compare and contrast farm animals. (e.g., Do they have four legs or two legs? Do they lay eggs or are they born alive?)

3. Continue singing the Farm Animals song, pointing to the cards in the pocket chart each time. Remind students that they can use these words in their writing.

4. Use the Barn Mini Book (pages 148–150) for guided or independent writing (see page 9). Encourage students to incorporate new information and ideas they have acquired since beginning the unit.

5. Make the Farm Animals Finger Puppets (page 151) and act out farm stories. Encourage students to write about their experiences.

My Story About _____

By _____

Farm Animals Mini Book

Materials

- Farm Animals Mini Book patterns (pages 149 and 150)
- red construction paper
- white paper
- scissors
- stapler

Assembly Directions

1. Copy pages 149 and 150 (one of each page per student) onto red construction paper and cut out the barn shapes to create the front and back covers of the Farm Animals Mini Books.

2. Make copies of the barn pattern (page 150) on white paper and cut them out to make the inside pages of the mini books. For early writers, two pages per book will probably be sufficient. For more experienced writers, increase the number of pages.

3. Assemble the books and staple them together.

Farm Animals Finger Puppets

Materials

- Farm Animals Finger Puppet Patterns (page 151)
- crayons or markers
- scissors
- glue and tape
- various craft materials (cotton balls, feathers, fake fur, yarn, google eyes, etc.)
- heavy white paper

Preparation

- Make copies of the Farm Animals Finger Puppet Patterns page on heavy white paper (one per student).

Assembly Directions

1. Give each student a copy of the Farm Animals Finger Puppet Patterns. Tell them they can color the animals. Show students how to cut the puppets out along the thick lines.

2. Let students decorate their puppets by using glue to attach craft materials. Try gluing cotton balls onto the sheep, feathers onto the chicken, and use yarn to make the horse's mane. Reinforce each puppet by placing a piece of tape on the back of the finger strip.

3. Complete the puppets by taping the ends of the finger loops together.

4. Act out the Farm Animals song or let students make up farm stories and act them out.

5. Encourage students to write about their experiences.

Farm Animals Mini Book

Cover

Farm Animals

by _____

Farm Animals Mini Book *(cont.)*

Back Cover and Inside Pages

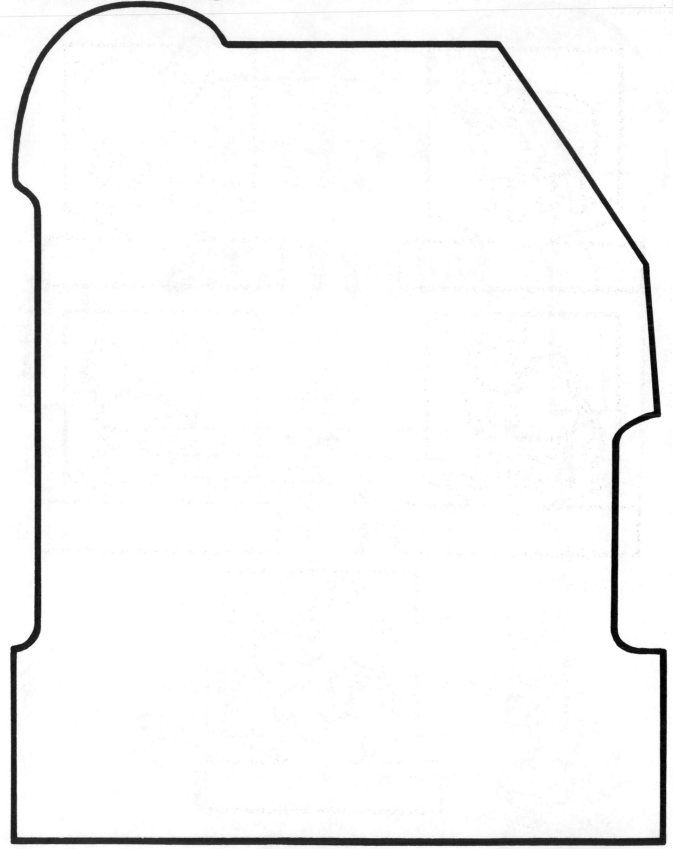

Farm Animals Finger Puppets

Patterns

Make **one** copy of this page.

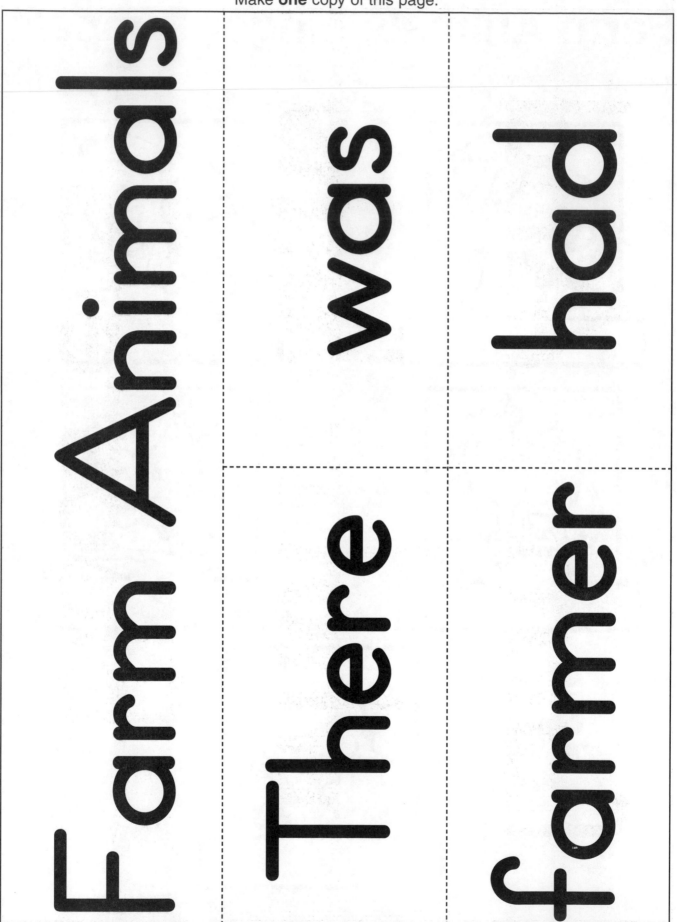

Farm Animals

was

had

There

farmer

Make **one** copy of this page.

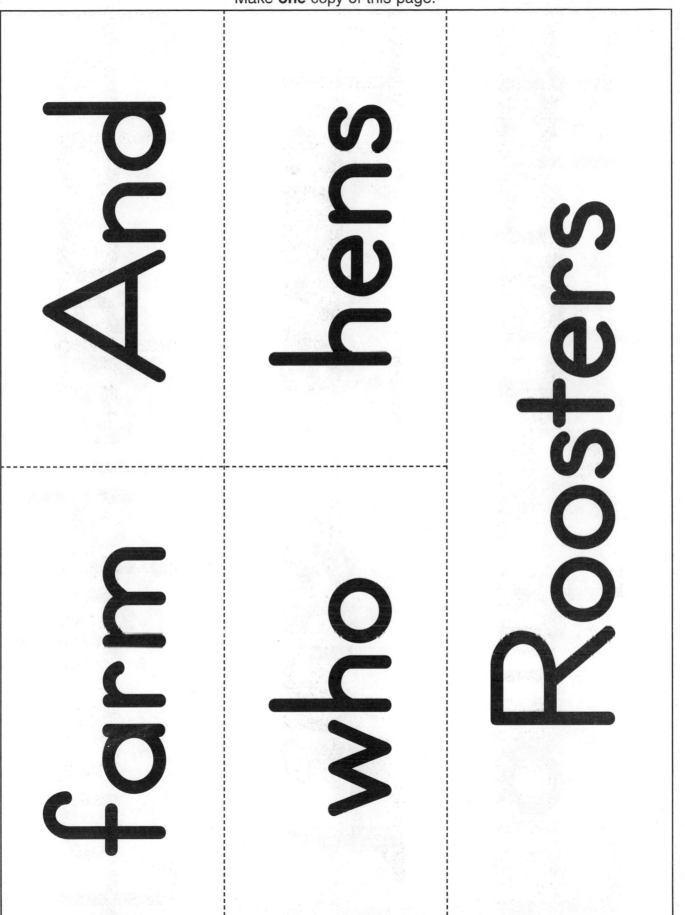

And

hens

Roosters

farm

who

Make **one** copy of this page.

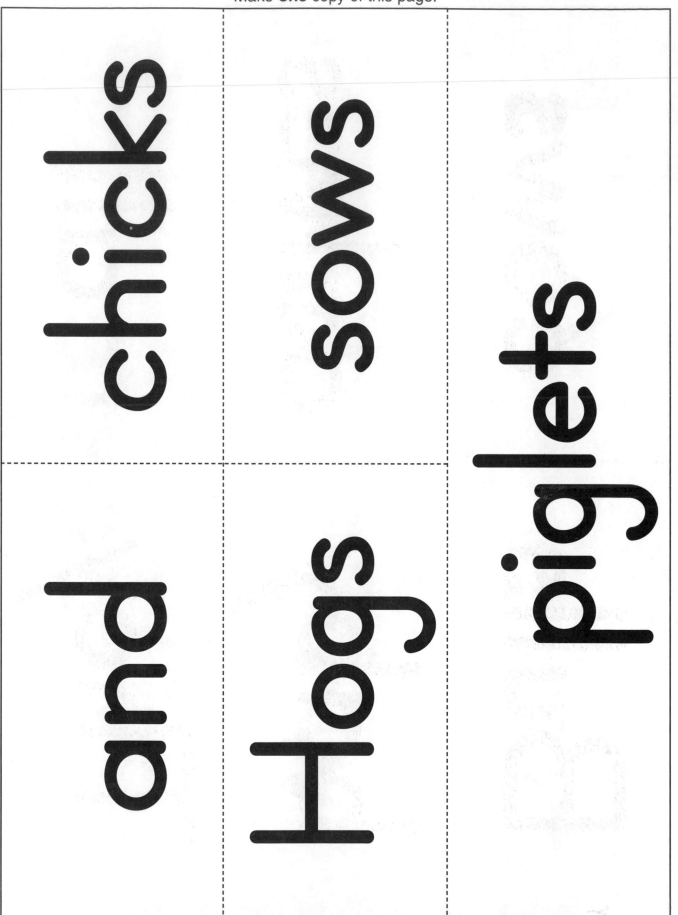

chicks

sows

piglets

and

Hogs

Make **one** copy of this page.

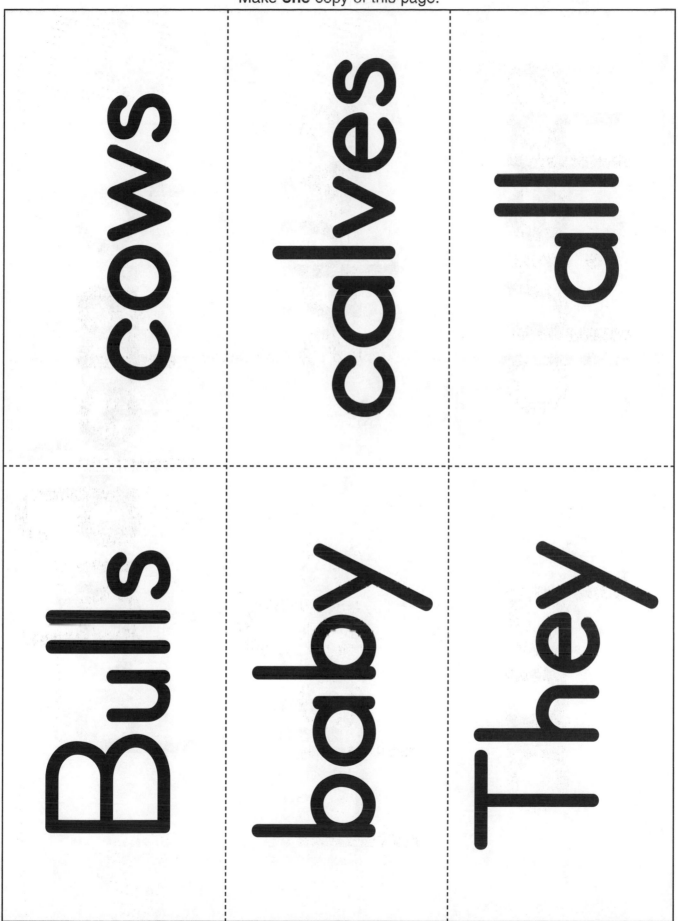

cows

calves

all

Bulls

baby

They

Make **two** copies of this page.

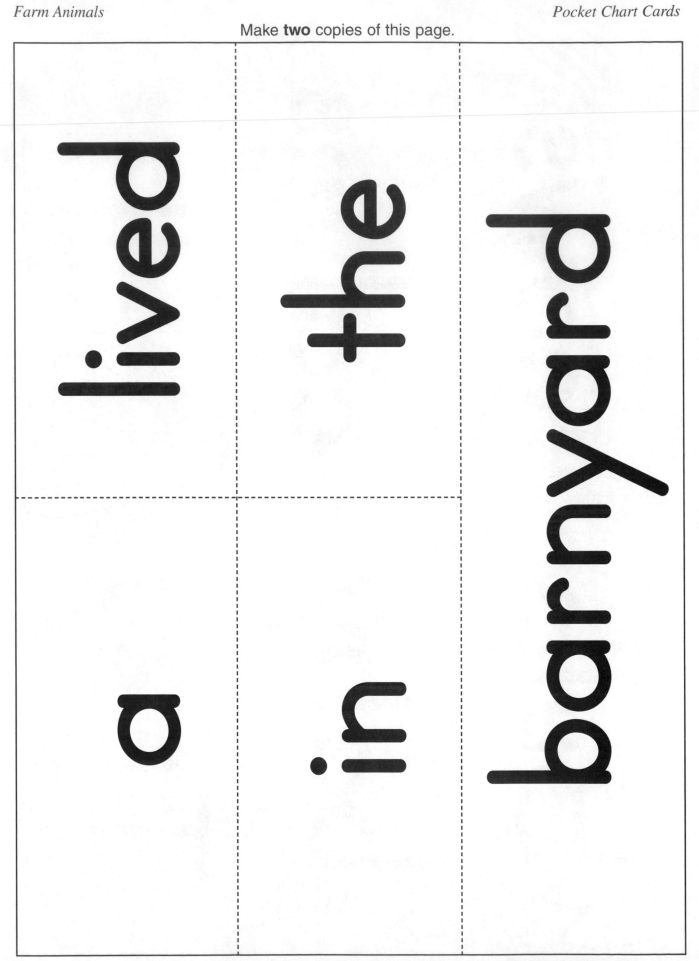

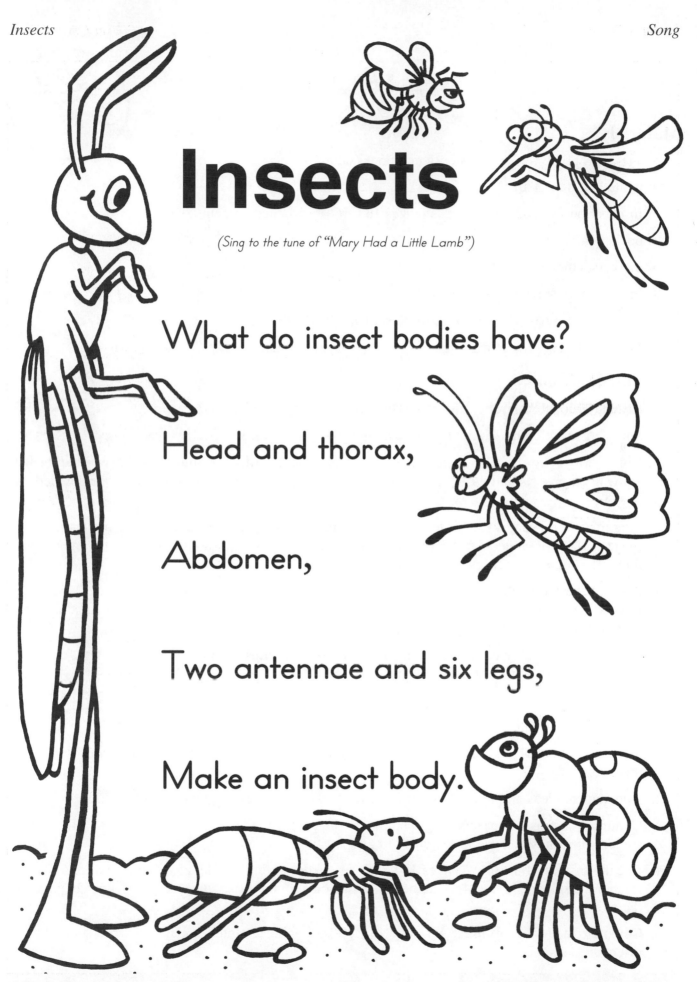

Insects

(Sing to the tune of "Mary Had a Little Lamb")

What do insect bodies have?

Head and thorax,

Abdomen,

Two antennae and six legs,

Make an insect body.

Insects

Materials

- age-appropriate fiction and nonfiction books about insects
- white board or chart paper and markers
- Insects Song Pocket Chart Cards (pages 163–168) laminated and cut apart
- pocket chart
- markers, colored pencils, and crayons
- Insects Story Writing Page for each child (page 159)
- assembled Insects Mini Book for each student (pages 160–162)
- Make an Insect project materials (page 160) for each student

head

thorax

abdomen

Unit Introduction

1. Read a fictional story about insects. Discuss the setting, characters, and plot.

2. Share a nonfiction book about insects, pointing out interesting facts.

3. Brainstorm. Write *Insects* at the top of a chart or white board. Ask students to share what they know about insects and write down their responses. Use the shared writing technique detailed on page 9.

4. Sing the Insects song while pointing to each of the words on the pocket chart. Picture cards (page 168) are included for the key vocabulary words. You may want to highlight the indicated body parts on each card by coloring it.

5. Pass out the Story Writing Page. Encourage students to write or draw their own stories about insects. You can use this time to do some guided writing with small groups or have the children write independently (see page 9).

6. Spend time with each child discussing his or her story or illustration. You will find tips for transcribing and editing students' stories on page 10.

Unit Activities

1. Continue sharing the fiction book about insects that you read during the unit introduction. Reread the nonfiction book and discuss interesting facts. Introduce additional books about insects during the week.

2. Add student ideas and new facts about insects to the brainstorming board.

3. Continue singing the Insects song, pointing to the cards in the pocket chart each time. Remind students that they can use these words in their writing.

4. Use the Insects Mini Book (pages 160–162) for guided or independent writing (see page 9). Encourage students to incorporate new information and ideas they have acquired since beginning the unit.

5. Complete the Make an Insect Art Project (page 160) and encourage students to write about their insects.

My Story About _____

By _____

Insects Mini Book

Materials

- Insects Mini Book patterns (pages 161 and 162)
- colored construction paper
- white paper
- scissors
- stapler

Assembly Directions

1. Copy pages 161 and 162 (one of each page per student) onto colored construction paper and cut out the insect shapes to create the front and back covers of the Insects Mini Books.

2. Make copies of the insect pattern (page 162) on white paper and cut them out to make the inside pages of the mini books. For early writers, two pages per book will probably be sufficient. For more experienced writers, increase the number of pages.

3. Assemble the books and staple them together.

Make an Insect Art Project

Materials

- play clay
- toothpicks
- craft sticks or chenille stems
- googly eyes or beads
- various craft materials (feathers, glitter, etc.)
- colored construction paper
- scissors

Directions

1. Show students how to roll the play clay into balls. Each student should make three balls for the head, thorax, and abdomen of their insect. Use toothpicks to hold the parts together.

2. Have students add six legs (craft sticks or chenille stems) to the thorax and two eyes (googly eyes or beads), and let them use the craft materials (feathers, glitter, etc.) to decorate their insect. They can cut the colored construction paper to make wings.

3. Display the made-up insects in the classroom and encourage students to write about them.

Insects Mini Book

Cover

Insects Mini Book *(cont.)*

Back Cover and Inside Pages

162

Make **one** copy of this page.

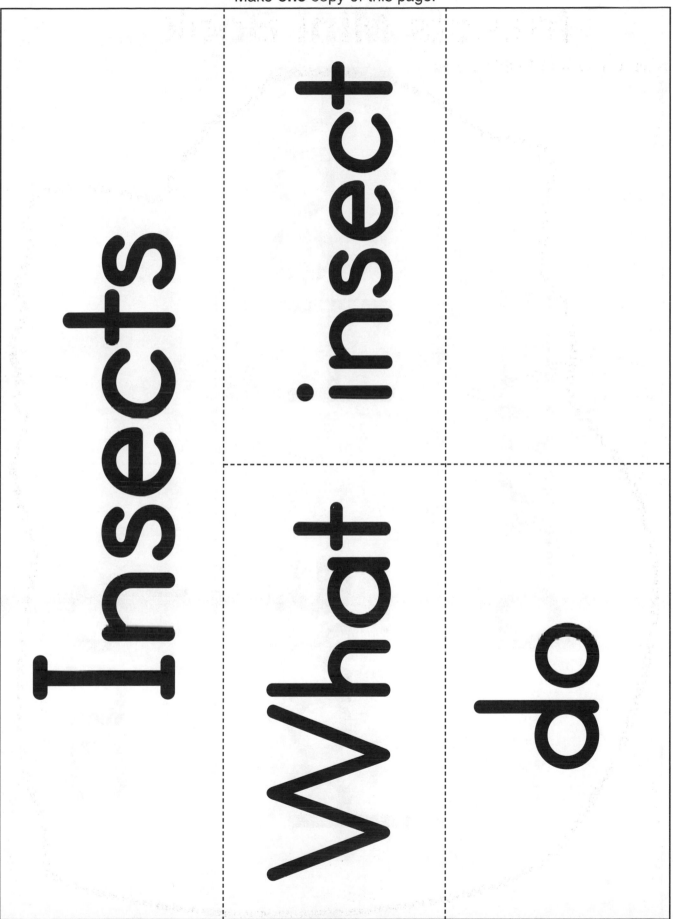

Insects

insect

What

do

Make **one** copy of this page.

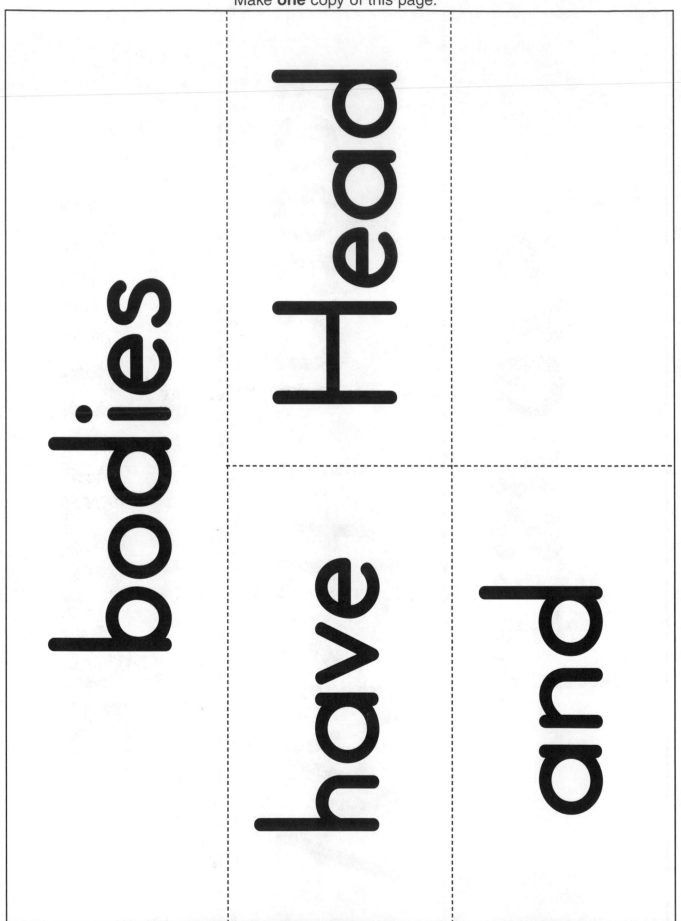

bodies

Head

have

and

Make **one** copy of this page.

thorax

antennae

Abdomen

Make **one** copy of this page.

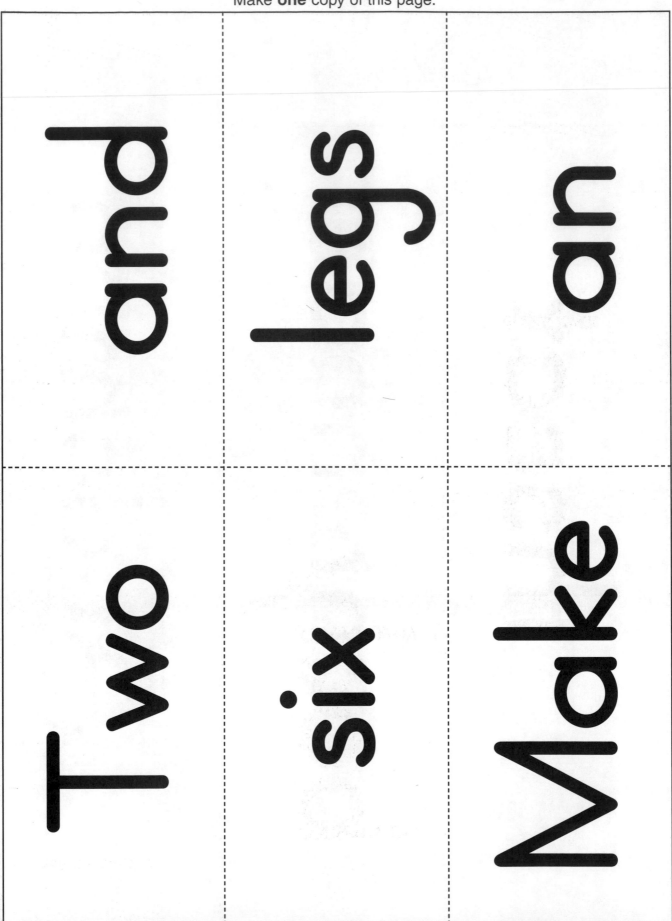

and	legs	an
Two	six	Make

Make **one** copy of this page.

insect

body

Make **one** copy of this page.

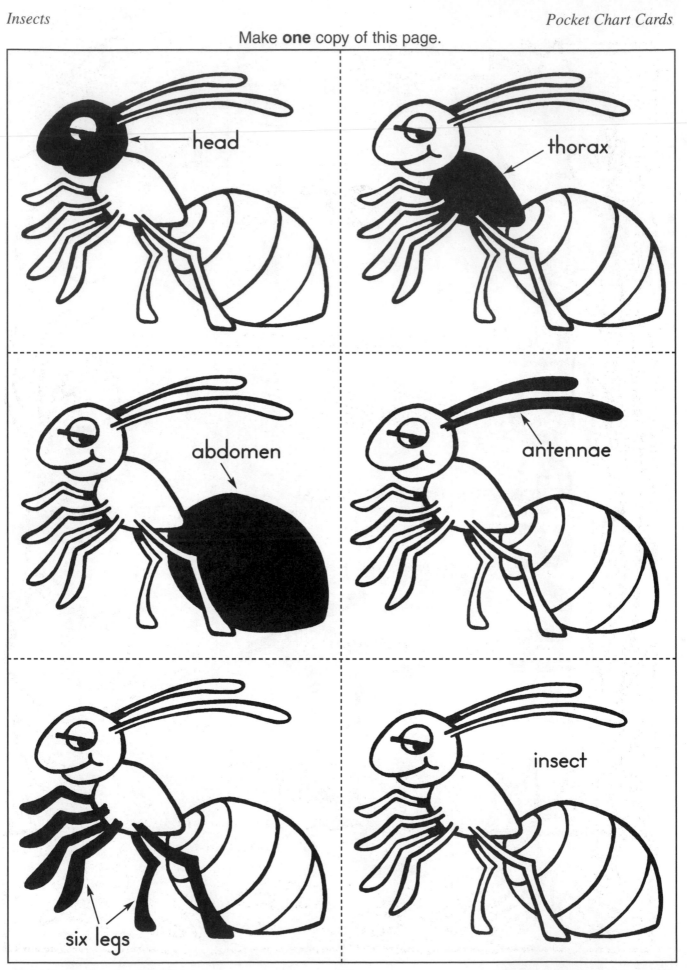

head

thorax

abdomen

antennae

six legs

insect

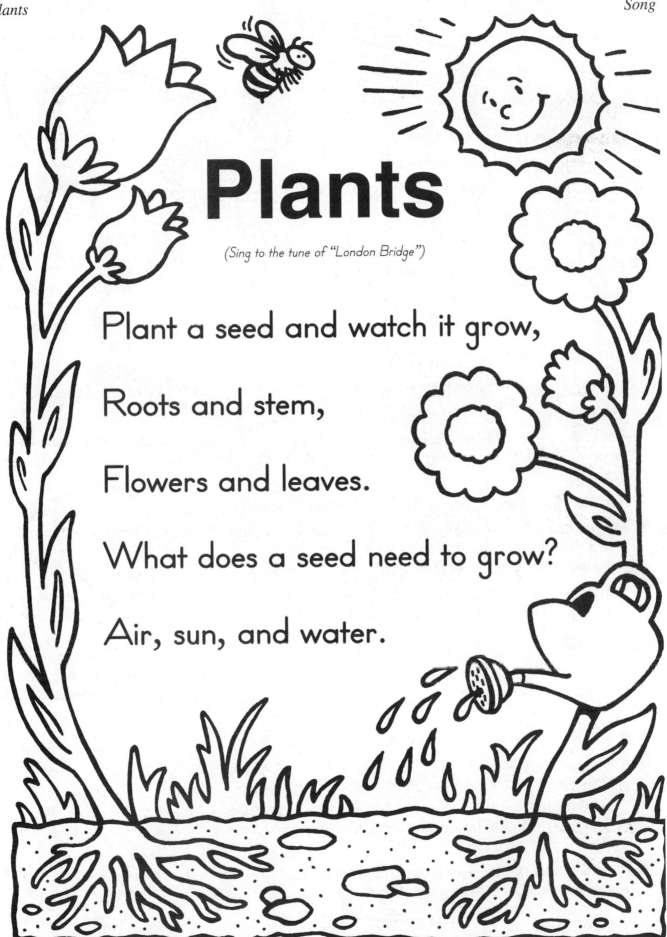

Plants

(Sing to the tune of "London Bridge")

Plant a seed and watch it grow,

Roots and stem,

Flowers and leaves.

What does a seed need to grow?

Air, sun, and water.

Plants

Materials

- age-appropriate fiction and nonfiction books about plants
- white board or chart paper and markers
- Plants Song Pocket Chart Cards (pages 177–180) laminated and cut apart
- pocket chart
- markers, colored pencils, and crayons
- Plants Story Writing Page for each child (page 171)
- assembled Plants Mini Book for each student (pages 172–174)
- Plant Parts and labels page (pages 175–176) and project materials (page 172) for each student

Unit Introduction

1. Read a fictional story about plants. Discuss the setting, characters, and plot.
2. Share a nonfiction book about plants, pointing out interesting facts.
3. Brainstorm. Write *Plants* at the top of a chart or white board. Ask students to share what they know about plants and write down their responses. Use the shared writing technique detailed on page 9.
4. Sing the Plants song while pointing to each of the words on the pocket chart.
5. Pass out the Story Writing Page. Encourage students to write or draw their own stories about plants. You can use this time to do some guided writing with small groups or have the children write independently (see page 9).
6. Spend time with each child discussing his or her story or illustration. You will find tips for transcribing and editing students' stories on page 10.

Unit Activities

1. Continue sharing the fiction book about plants that you read during the unit introduction. Reread the nonfiction book and discuss interesting facts. Introduce additional books about plants during the week.
2. Add student ideas and new facts about plants to the brainstorming board.
3. Continue singing the Plants song, pointing to the cards in the pocket chart each time. Remind students that they can use these words in their writing.
4. Use the Plants Mini Book (pages 172–174) for guided or independent writing (see page 9). Encourage students to incorporate new information and ideas they have acquired since beginning the unit.
5. Complete the Plant Parts art project (pages 172, 175–176), display them in the classroom, and encourage students to write about their work.

My Story About _____

By _____

Plants Mini Book

Materials

- Plants Mini Book patterns (pages 173 and 174)
- colored construction paper
- white paper   • scissors   • stapler

Assembly Directions

1. Copy pages 173 and 174 (one of each page per student) onto colored construction paper and cut out the flower shapes to create the front and back covers of the Plants Mini Books.

2. Make copies of the flower pattern (page 174) on white paper and cut them out to make the inside pages of the mini books. For early writers, two pages per book will probably be sufficient. For more experienced writers, increase the number of pages.

3. Assemble the books and staple them together.

Plant Parts Project

Materials

- Plant Parts and Labels (pages 175 and 176)
- white construction paper
- large sheets of light blue construction paper (one per student)
- brown paper bags (or brown construction or tissue paper)
- crayons or markers
- glue   • seeds   • scissors

Preparation

- Copy the Plant Parts and Labels pages (pages 175 and 176) on white construction paper (one per student).

Directions

1. Review the parts of a plant (roots, stem, leaves, flower, seeds) and what plants need to grow (soil, sun, air, water).

2. Give each student a large sheet of light blue construction paper and have them make soil for their plants by pasting ripped pieces of brown paper bag (or brown construction or tissue paper) over the bottom third of their papers.

3. Give each student a copy of the Plant Parts and Labels page. Have students color and cut out the plant parts and labels.

4. Show students how to glue the plant parts onto their construction paper to make a plant (see sample above). Remind them to put the roots in the ground and the stem, leaves, and flower on top.

5. Let students glue seeds to the centers of their flowers. They can add details like the sun, a watering can or hose, and some insects with crayons or markers.

6. Display students' completed plants in the classroom and encourage them to write about their work.

Plants Mini Book

Cover

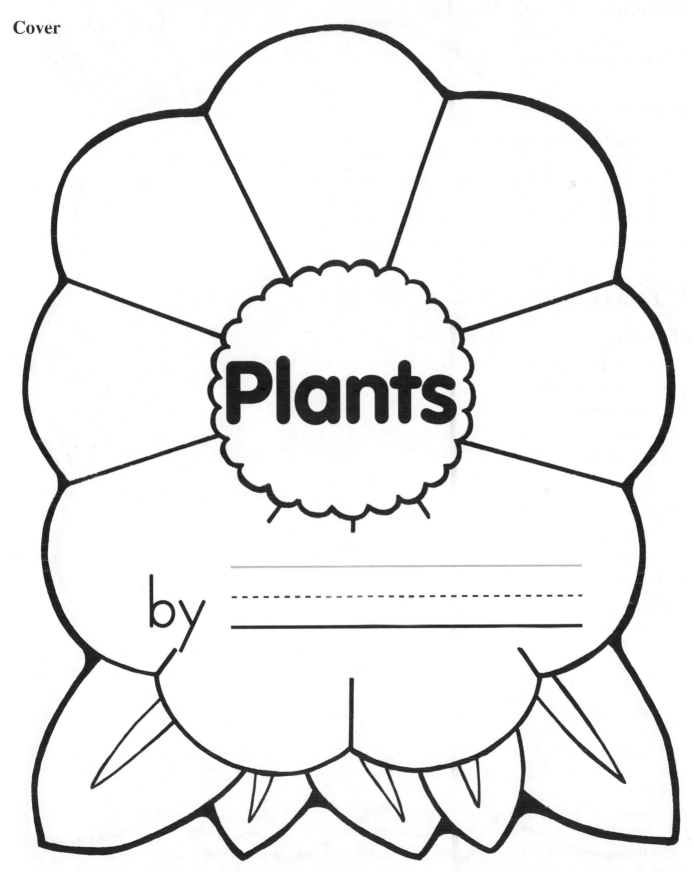

Plants

by _____

Plants Mini Book *(cont.)*

Back Cover and Inside Pages

Plant Parts

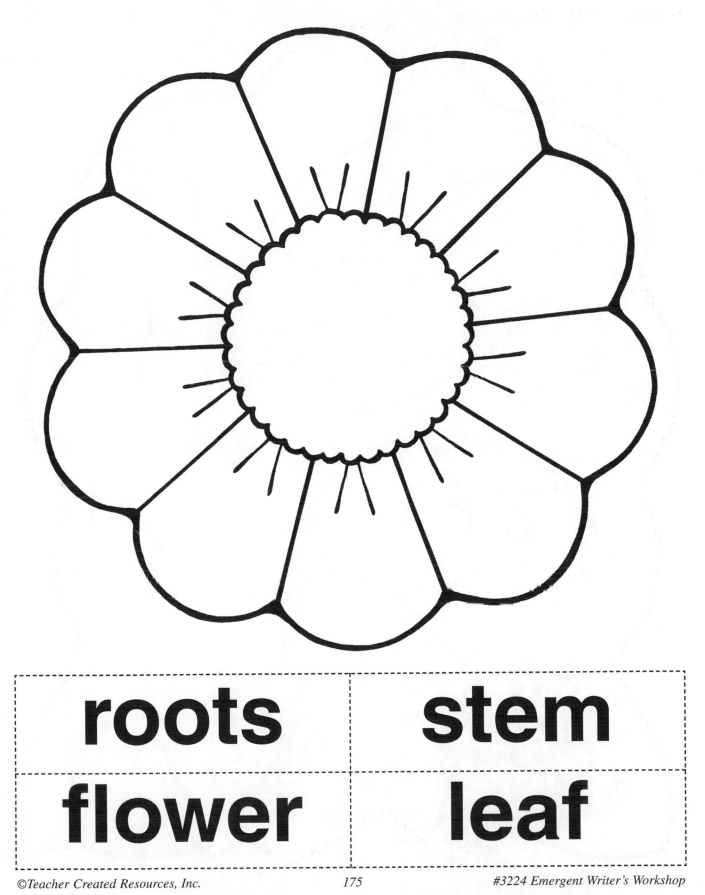

roots	stem
flower	leaf

Plant Parts *(cont.)*

Make **one** copy of this page.

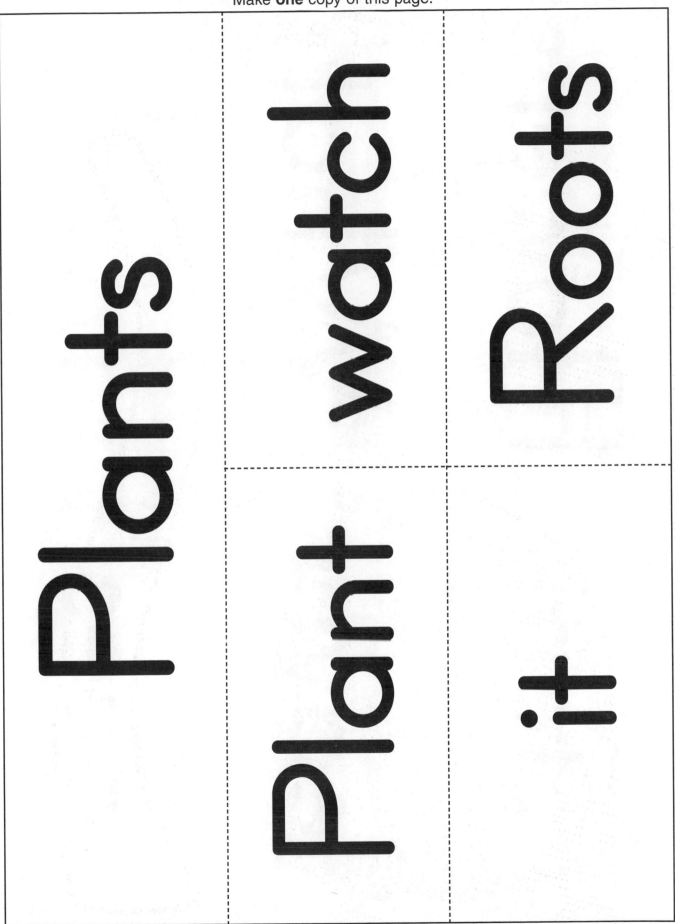

Plants

watch

Roots

Plant

it

Make **one** copy of this page.

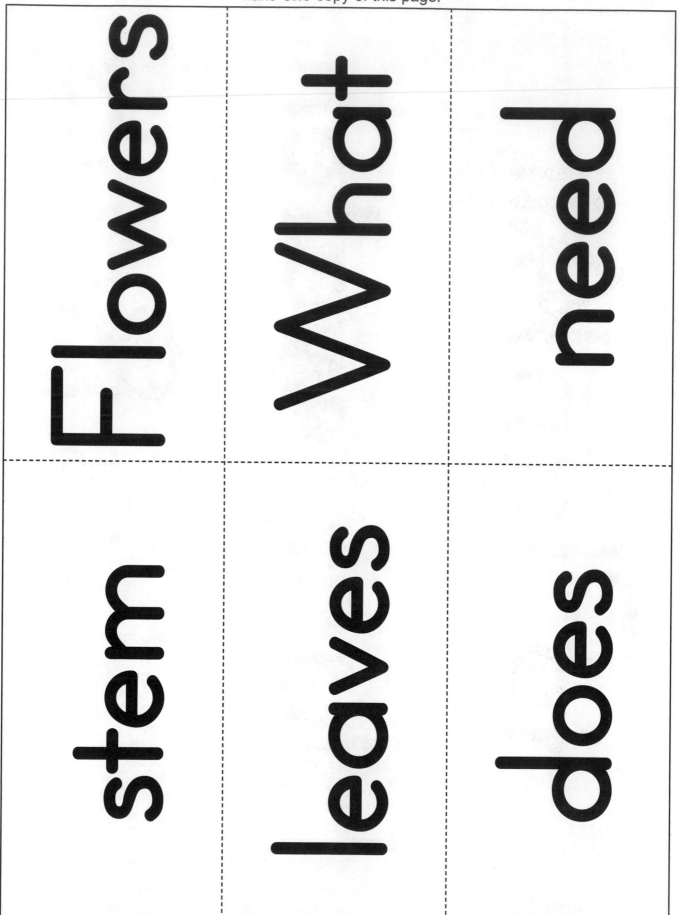

Flowers

What

need

stem

leaves

does

Make **one** copy of this page.

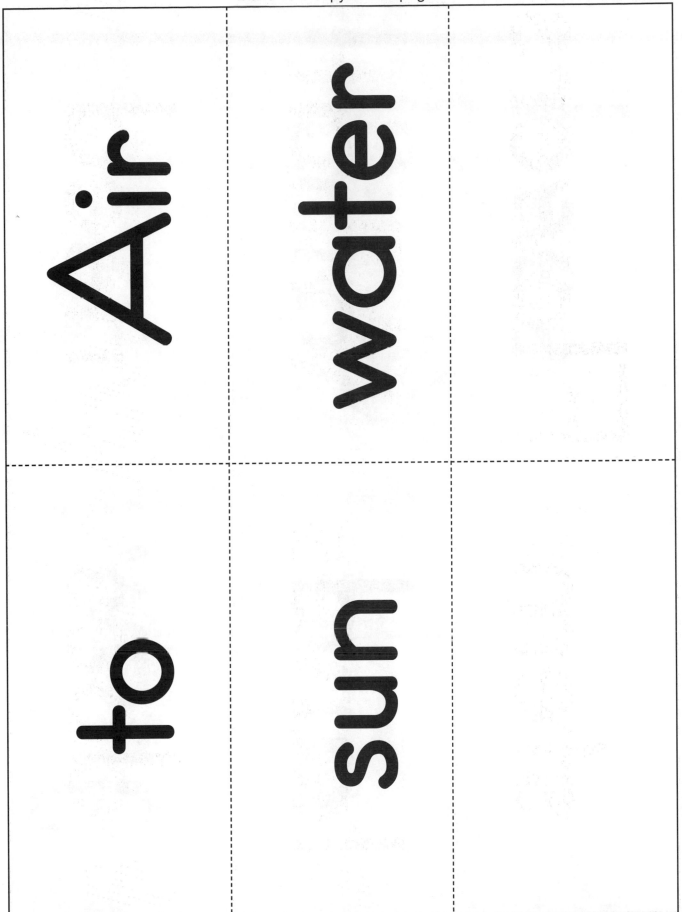

Make **two** copies of this page.

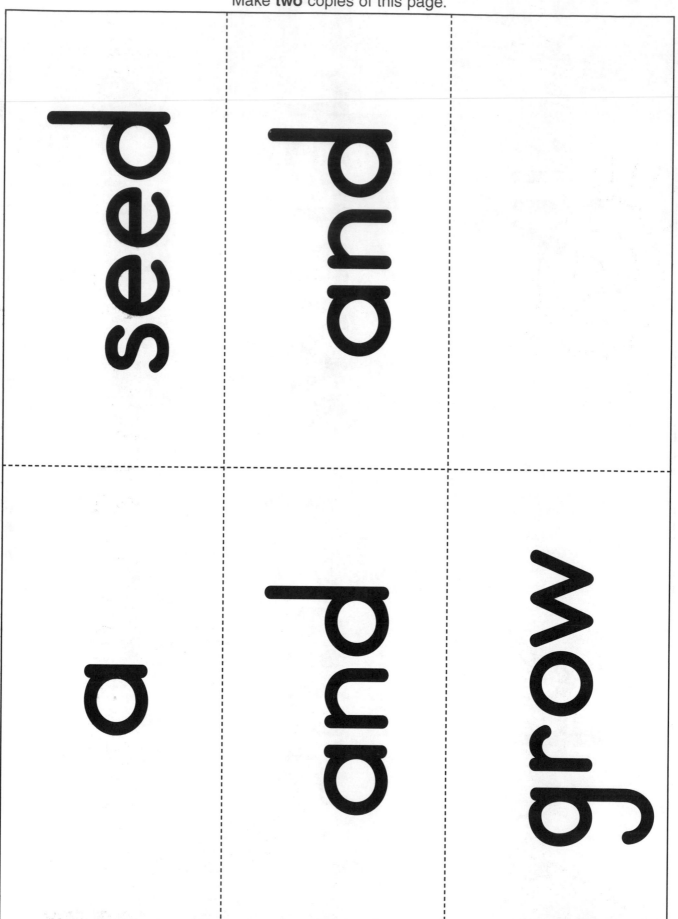

seed

and

a

and

grow

The Weather

(Sing to the tune of "The More We Get Together")

Let's talk about the weather,

The weather, the weather,

Let's talk about the weather,

It's _____ out today.

Weather

Materials

- age-appropriate fiction and nonfiction books about weather
- white board or chart paper and markers
- Weather Song Pocket Chart Cards (pages 189–192) laminated and cut apart
- pocket chart
- markers, colored pencils, and crayons
- Weather Story Writing Page for each child (page 183)
- assembled Weather Mini Book for each student (pages 184–186)
- What Will You Wear? Paper Doll and Clothing (pages 187–188) and project materials (page 184) for each student

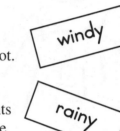

Unit Introduction

1. Read a fictional story about weather. Discuss the setting, characters, and plot.

2. Share a nonfiction book about weather, pointing out interesting facts.

3. Brainstorm. Write *Weather* at the top of a chart or white board. Ask students to share what they know about weather and write down their responses. Use the shared writing technique detailed on page 9.

4. Sing the Weather song while pointing to each of the words on the pocket chart. Change the weather word in the last line (sunny, cloudy, rainy, windy, snowy) each time you sing the song.

5. Pass out the Story Writing Page. Encourage students to write or draw their own stories about weather. You can use this time to do some guided writing with small groups or have the children write independently (see page 9).

6. Spend time with each child discussing his or her story or illustration. You will find tips for transcribing and editing students' stories on page 10.

Unit Activities

1. Continue sharing the fiction book about weather that you read during the unit introduction. Reread the nonfiction book and discuss interesting facts. Introduce additional books about weather during the week.

2. Add student ideas and new facts about weather to the brainstorming board.

3. Continue singing the Weather song, pointing to the cards in the pocket chart each time. Remind students that they can use these words in their writing.

4. Use the Weather Mini Book (pages 184–186) for guided or independent writing (see page 9). Encourage students to incorporate new information and ideas they have acquired since beginning the unit.

5. Complete the What Will You Wear? art project on page 184, display them in the classroom, and encourage students to write about their work.

My Story About _____

By _____

Weather Mini Book

Materials

- Weather Mini Book patterns (pages 185 and 186)
- white or gray construction paper
- white paper
- scissors
- stapler

Assembly Directions

1. Copy pages 185 and 186 (one of each page per student) onto white or gray construction paper and cut out the cloud shapes to create the front and back covers of the Weather Mini Books.

2. Make copies of the cloud pattern (page 186) on white paper and cut them out to make the inside pages of the mini books. For early writers, two pages per book will probably be sufficient. For more experienced writers, increase the number of pages.

3. Assemble the books and staple them together.

What Will You Wear?

Materials

- What Will You Wear? Paper Doll and Clothing pages (pages 187–188)
- large sheets of construction paper (one per student)
- crayons or markers
- glue
- scissors

Preparation

- Make copies of the What Will You Wear? Paper Doll and Clothing pages (one of each page per student).

Directions

1. Ask each student to choose his or her favorite type of weather. Give each student a large piece of construction paper and let them create a weather scene using crayons or markers. For example, if their favorite kind of weather is sunny, they might draw a beach scene or a park. If their favorite kind of weather is rainy, they could draw clouds, rain, and puddles.

2. Give each student a copy of the What Will You Wear? Paper Doll and Clothing pages. Let students color the paper dolls and add details (hair, skin color, etc.) to make it look like them. Help them cut out the paper dolls.

3. Tell students that they will be putting their paper dolls into their weather scenes. Ask them to color and cut out the clothing that they would wear for their favorite type of weather.

4. Have students glue their paper dolls into their weather scenes and "dress" the dolls in the proper clothes.

5. Encourage students to write captions for or stories about their weather scenes.

Weather Mini Book

Cover

Weather Mini Book *(cont.)*

Back Cover and Inside Pages

What Will You Wear?

Paper Doll

What Will You Wear? *(cont.)*

Clothing

Make **one** copy of this page.

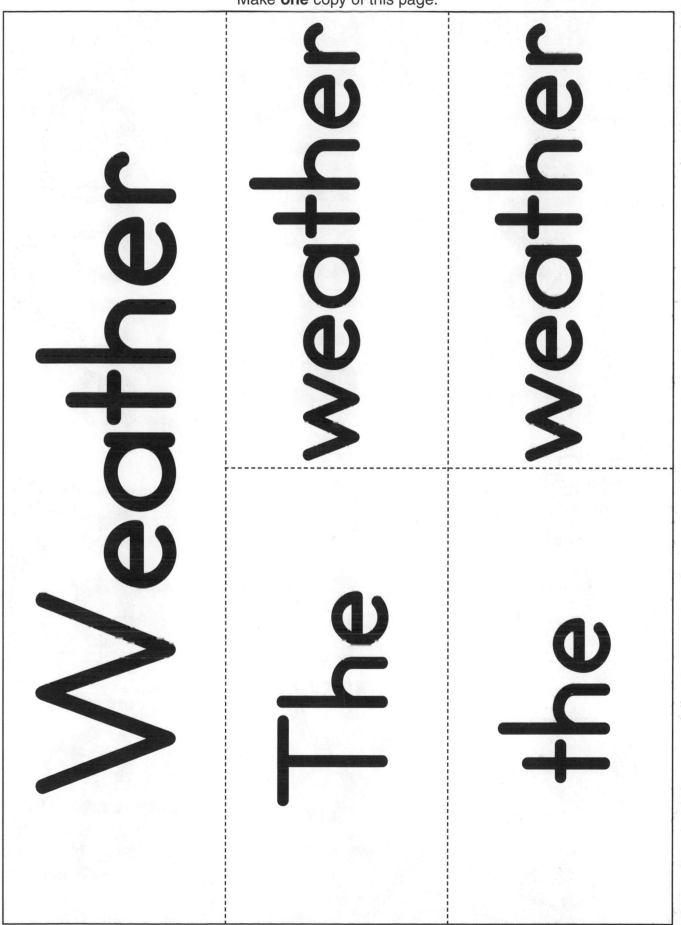

Make **one** copy of this page.

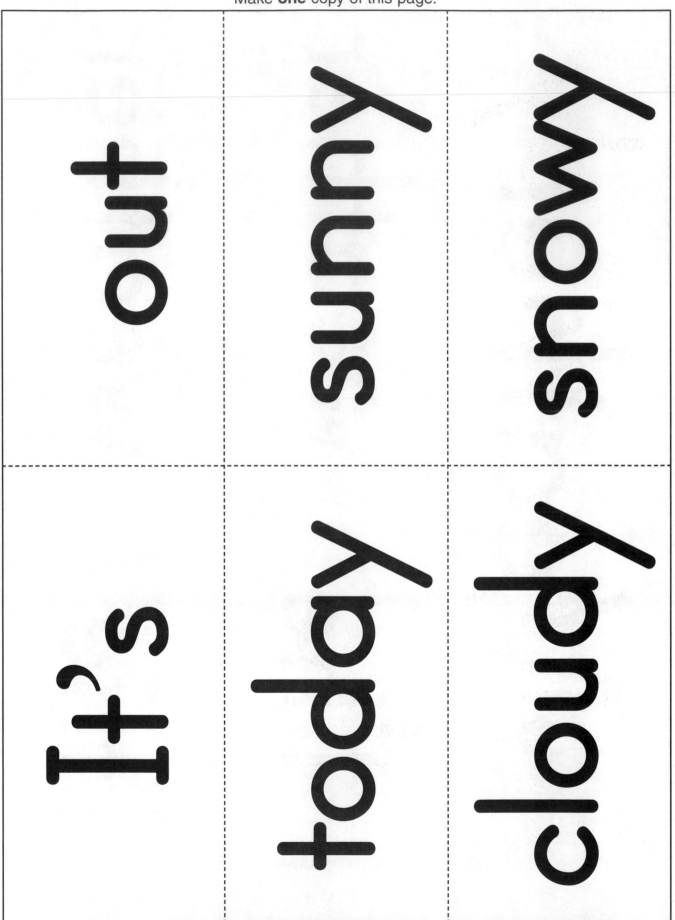

out

sunny

snowy

It's

today

cloudy

Make **one** copy of this page.

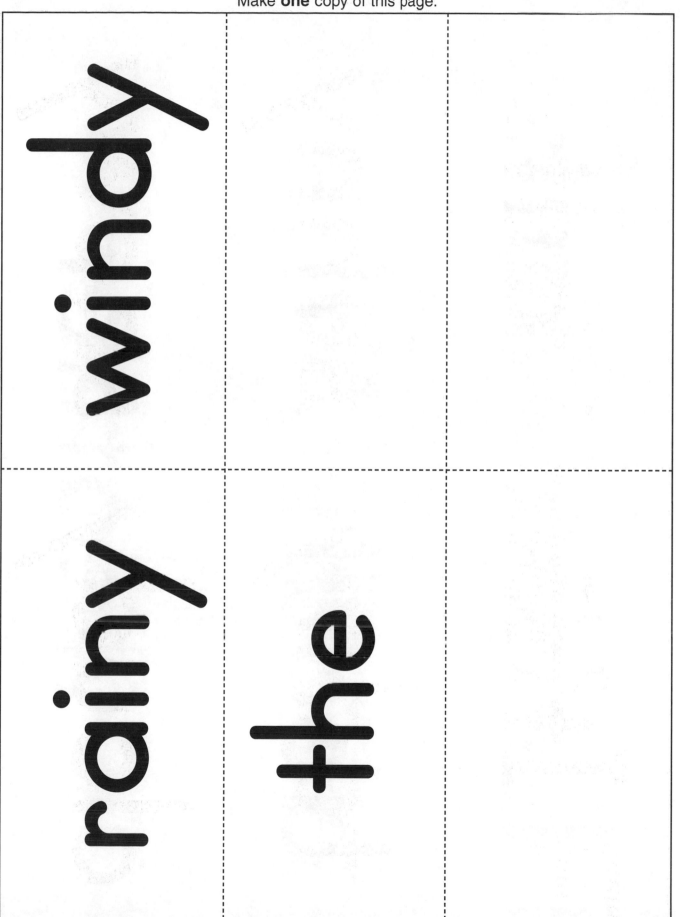

windy

rainy

the

Make **two** copies of this page.

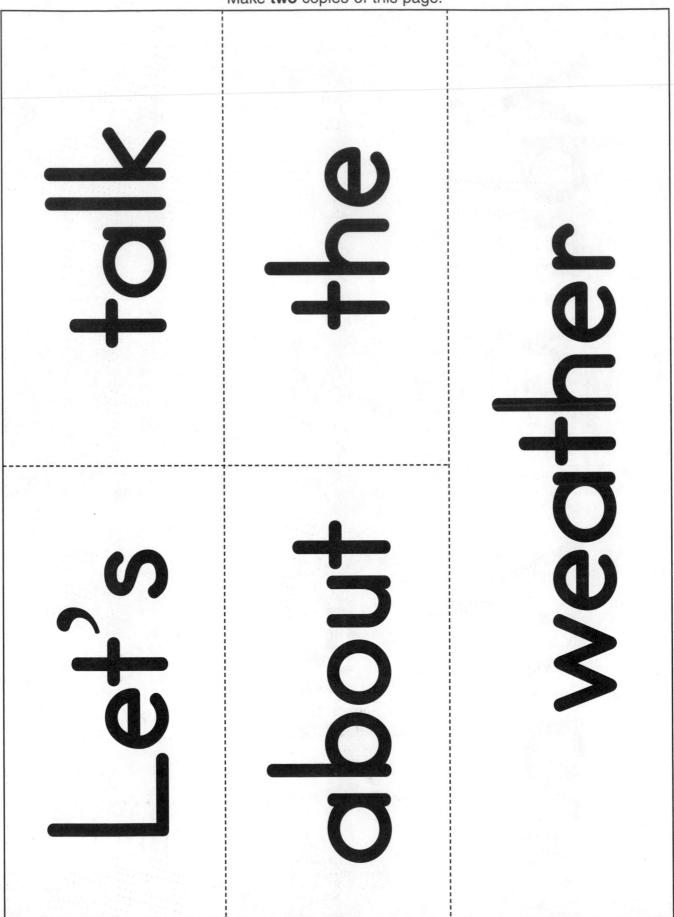

talk

the

weather

Let's

about

Summer

(Sing to the tune of "If You're Happy and You Know It")

Oh, it's fun to splash and swim in summertime.

Oh, it's fun to splash and swim in summertime.

We will all be keeping cool,

At the beach or in the pool,

Oh, it's fun to splash and swim in summertime.

Summer

Materials

- age-appropriate fiction and nonfiction books about summer
- white board or chart paper and markers
- Summer Song Pocket Chart Cards (pages 200–203) laminated and cut apart
- pocket chart
- markers, colored pencils, and crayons
- Summer Story Writing Page for each child (page 195)
- assembled Summer Mini Book for each student (pages 196–198)
- Summer Sun Pattern (page 199) and project materials (page 196) for each student

Unit Introduction

1. Read a fictional story about summer. Discuss the setting, characters, and plot.

2. Share a nonfiction book about summer, pointing out interesting facts.

3. Brainstorm. Write *Summer* at the top of a chart or white board. Ask students to share what they know about summertime and write down their responses. Use the shared writing technique detailed on page 9.

4. Sing the Summer song while pointing to each of the words on the pocket chart.

5. Pass out the Story Writing Page. Encourage students to write or draw their own stories about summer. You can use this time to do some guided writing with small groups or have the children write independently (see page 9).

6. Spend time with each child discussing his or her story or illustration. You will find tips for transcribing and editing students' stories on page 10.

Unit Activities

1. Continue sharing the fiction book about summer that you read during the unit introduction. Reread the nonfiction book and discuss interesting facts. Introduce additional books about summer during the week.

2. Add student ideas and new facts about summer to the brainstorming board.

3. Continue singing the Summer song, pointing to the cards in the pocket chart each time. Remind students that they can use these words in their writing.

4. Use the Summer Mini Book (pages 196–198) for guided or independent writing (see page 9). Encourage students to incorporate new information and ideas they have acquired since beginning the unit.

5. Complete the Summer Sun Art Project (pages 196 and 199), display them in the classroom, and encourage students to write about their work.

My Story About _____

By _____

Summer Mini Book

Materials

- Summer Mini Book patterns (pages 197 and 198)
- yellow or orange construction paper
- white paper
- scissors
- stapler

Assembly Directions

1. Copy pages 197 and 198 (one of each page per student) onto yellow or orange construction paper and cut out the sun shapes to create the front and back covers of the Summer Mini Books.

2. Make copies of the sun pattern (page 198) on white paper and cut them out to make the inside pages of the mini books. For early writers, two pages per book will probably be sufficient. For more experienced writers, increase the number of pages.

3. Assemble the books and staple them together.

Summer Sun Art Project

Materials

- Sun pattern (page 199)
- large sheets of white (or other light colored) construction paper (one per student)
- scissors
- glue or paste
- yellow, orange, and red tempra or other washable paints
- pie plates or other shallow containers

Preparation

- Make copies of the Sun pattern (one per student).
- Put paint in shallow containers and prepare for finger painting.

Directions

1. Give each student a copy of the Sun pattern. Ask them to cut out the sun's face and glue it in the center of their piece of construction paper.

2. Show students how to dip their fingers in the paints and color the sun's face. Then show them how to make their handprints for the sun's rays (see illustration). You could have them make a pattern with the different color paints.

3. Encourage students to write captions for stories about their suns.

Summer Mini Book

Cover

by _____

Summer Mini Book

Back Cover and Inside Pages

Sun

Pattern

Make **one** copy of this page.

Summer

will

We

be

in

all

Make **one** copy of this page.

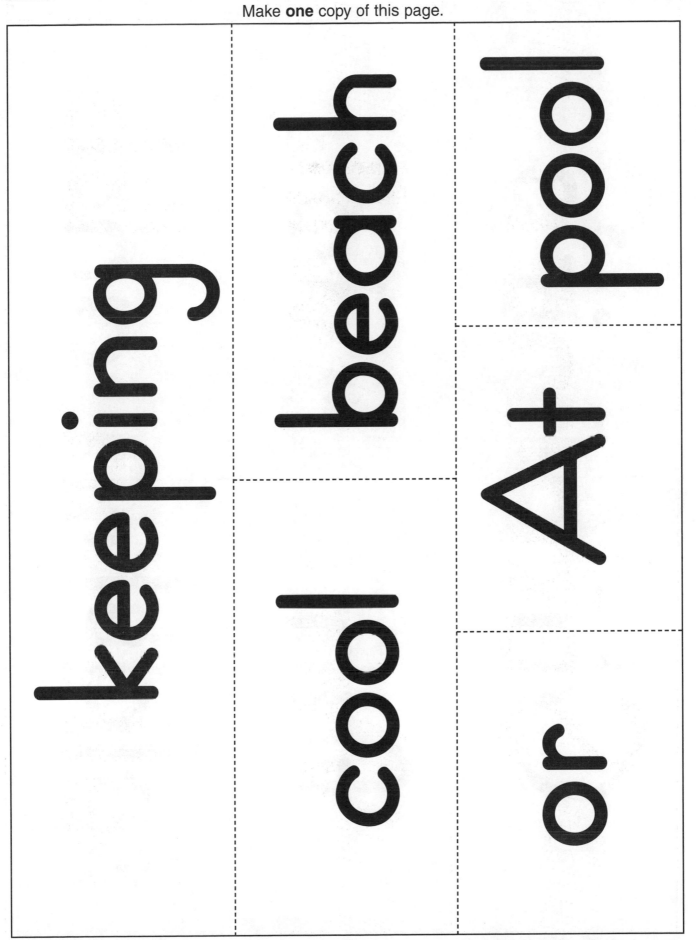

keeping

beach

pool

cool

A+

or

Make **three** copies of this page.

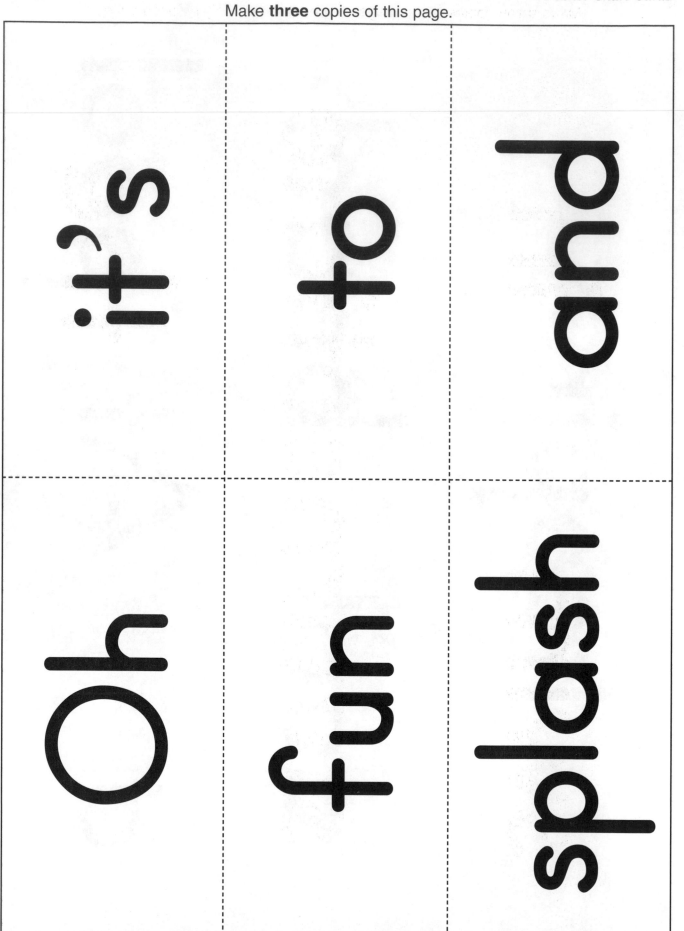

it's

to

and

Oh

fun

splash

Make **three** copies of this page. **Note:** 'the' will only be used once.

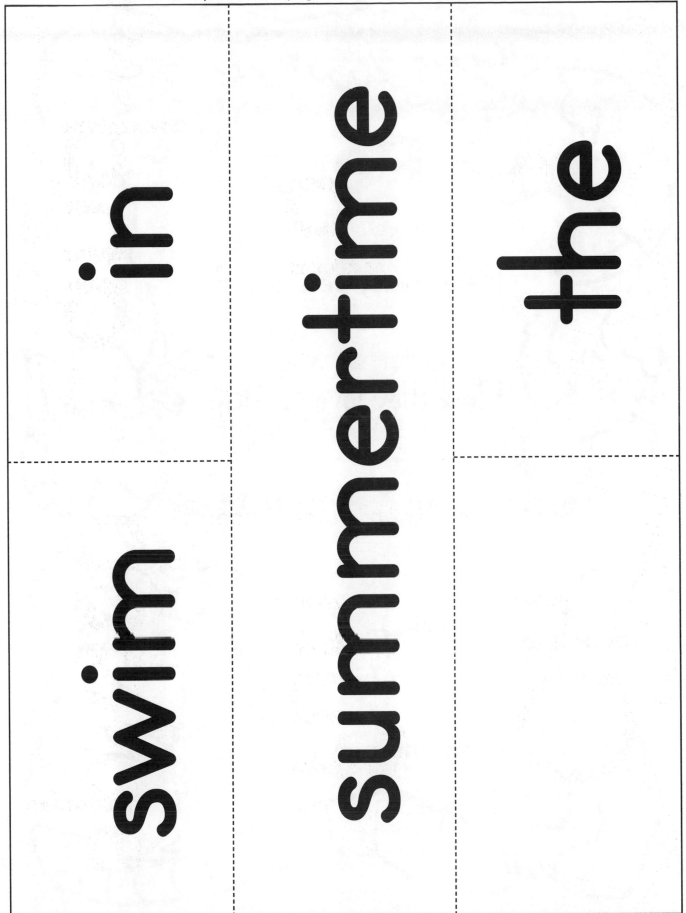

in

summertime

the

swim

Pets

(Sing to the tune of "Row, Row, Row Your Boat")

Pets, pets, pets are fun,

How they love to play.

Feed them, clean them,

Give them water,

Love them every day.

204

Pets

pets

play

fun

Materials

- age-appropriate fiction and nonfiction books about pets
- white board or chart paper and markers
- Pets Song Pocket Chart Cards (pages 210–213) laminated and cut apart
- pocket chart
- markers, colored pencils, and crayons
- Pets Story Writing Page for each child (page 206)
- assembled Pets Mini Book for each student (pages 207–209)
- Pet Rock Art Project materials (page 207) for each student

Unit Introduction

1. Read a fictional story about pets. Discuss the setting, characters, and plot.

2. Share a nonfiction book about pets, pointing out interesting facts.

3. Brainstorm. Write *Pets* at the top of a chart or white board. Ask students to share what they know about pets and write down their responses. Use the shared writing technique detailed on page 9.

4. Sing the Pets song while pointing to each of the words on the pocket chart.

5. Pass out the Story Writing Page. Encourage students to write or draw their own stories about pets. You can use this time to do some guided writing with small groups or have the children write independently (see page 9).

6. Spend time with each child discussing his or her story or illustration. You will find tips for transcribing and editing students' stories on page 10.

Unit Activities

1. Continue sharing the fiction book about pets that you read during the unit introduction. Reread the nonfiction book and discuss interesting facts. Introduce additional books about pets during the week.

2. Add student ideas and new facts about pets to the brainstorming board.

3. Continue singing the Pets song, pointing to the cards in the pocket chart each time. Remind students that they can use these words in their writing.

4. Use the Pets Mini Book (pages 207–209) for guided or independent writing (see page 9). Encourage students to incorporate new information and ideas they have acquired since beginning the unit.

5. Complete the Pet Rock Art Project (page 207) and encourage students to write about their new pets.

My Story About _____

By _____

Pets Mini Book

Materials

- Pets Mini Book patterns (pages 208 and 209)
- colored construction paper
- white paper
- scissors
- stapler

Assembly Directions

1. Copy pages 208 and 209 (one of each page per student) onto colored construction paper and cut out the doghouse shapes to create the front and back covers of the Pets Mini Books.

2. Make copies of the doghouse pattern (page 209) on white paper and cut them out to make the inside pages of the mini books. For early writers, two pages per book will probably be sufficient. For more experienced writers, increase the number of pages.

3. Assemble the books and staple them together.

Pet Rock Art Project

Materials

- smooth rocks, about the size of a child's palm (one per student)
- paints and paint brushes
- various craft materials (googly eyes, feathers, etc.)
- glue

Preparation

- Prepare for painting.

Directions

1. Tell students that they will be creating their own imaginary pets.

2. Give each student a rock. Tell them to paint the rocks any way they wish.

3. Let students add googly eyes, feathers, and other craft materials to make their pets special.

4. Encourage students to write about their new pets.

Pets Mini Book

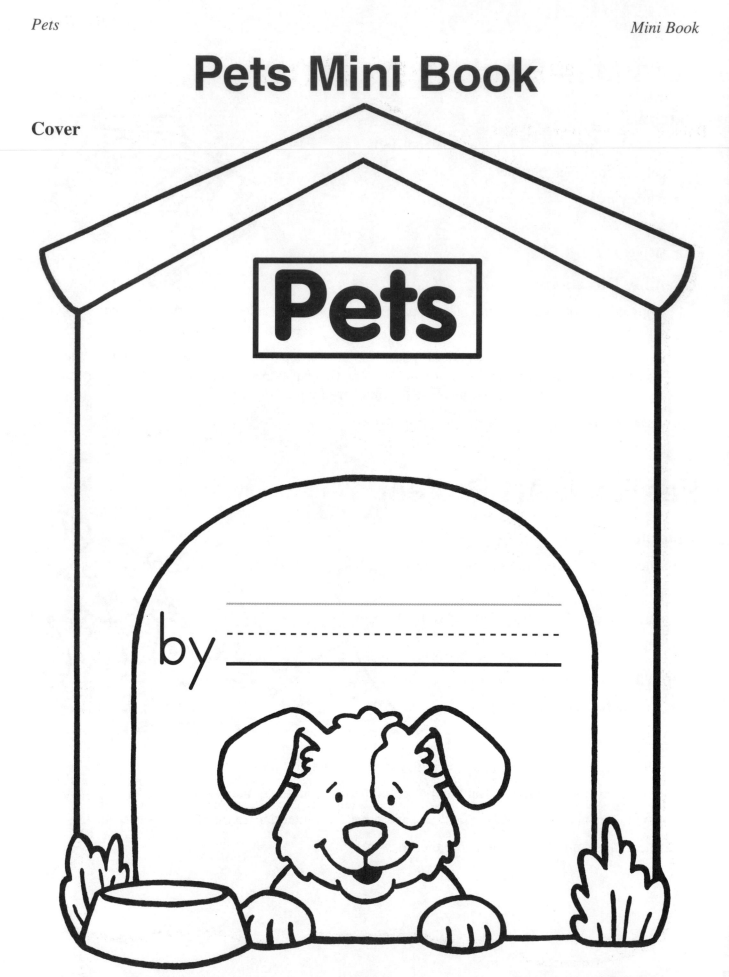

Pets

by _____

Pets Mini Book *(cont.)*

Back Cover and Inside Pages

Make **one** copy of this page.

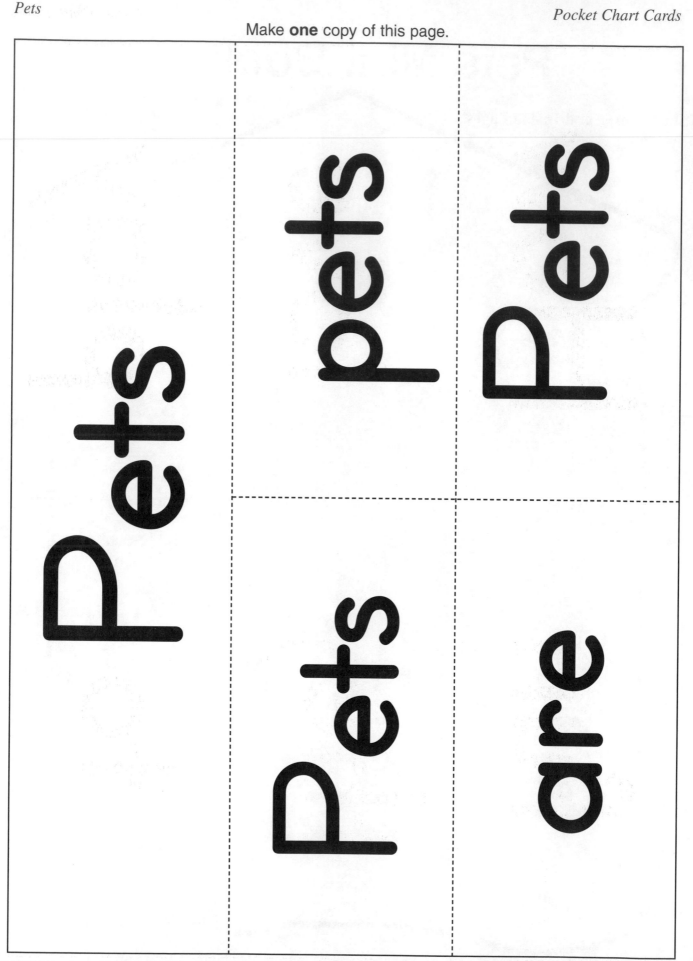

Make **one** copy of this page.

How

love

play

fun

they

to

Make **one** copy of this page.

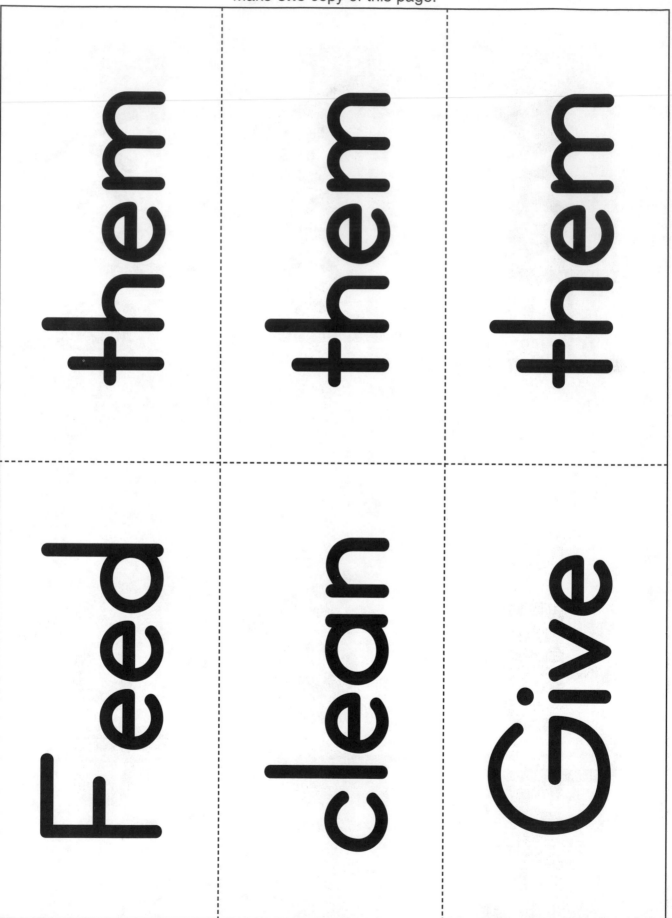

them

them

them

Feed

clean

Give

Make **one** copy of this page.

Love

every

water

them

day

Dinosaurs

(Sing to the tune of "Jingle Bells")

Dinosaurs,

Dinosaurs,

They ate plants or meat.

Lumbering on all four legs

Or running on two feet.

Oh!

Dinosaurs,

Dinosaurs,

They've all gone away.

They went extinct so long ago.

We find their bones today.

Dinosaurs

Materials

- age-appropriate fiction and nonfiction books about dinosaurs
- white board or chart paper and markers
- Dinosaurs Song Pocket Chart Cards (pages 220–226) laminated and cut apart
- pocket chart
- markers, colored pencils, and crayons
- Dinosaurs Story Writing Page for each child (page 216)
- assembled Dinosaurs Mini Book for each student (pages 217–219)
- Dinosaur Tracks project materials (page 217) for each student

Unit Introduction

1. Read a fictional story about dinosaurs. Discuss the setting, characters, and plot.
2. Share a nonfiction book about dinosaurs, pointing out interesting facts.
3. Brainstorm. Write *Dinosaurs* at the top of a chart or white board. Ask students to share what they know about dinosaurs and write down their responses. Use the shared writing technique detailed on page 9.
4. Sing the Dinosaurs song while pointing to each of the words on the pocket chart.
5. Pass out the Story Writing Page. Encourage students to write or draw their own stories about dinosaurs. You can use this time to do some guided writing with small groups or have the children write independently (see page 9).
6. Spend time with each child discussing his or her story or illustration. You will find tips for transcribing and editing students' stories on page 10.

Unit Activities

1. Continue sharing the fiction book about dinosaurs that you read during the unit introduction. Reread the nonfiction book and discuss interesting facts. Introduce additional books about dinosaurs during the week.
2. Add student ideas and new facts about dinosaurs to the brainstorming board.
3. Continue singing the Dinosaurs song, pointing to cards in the pocket chart each time. Remind students that they can use these words in their writing.
4. Use the Dinosaurs Mini Book (pages 217–219) for guided or independent writing (see page 9). Encourage students to incorporate new information and ideas they have acquired since beginning the unit.
5. Complete the Dinosaur Tracks Art Project (page 217) and encourage students to write about their art.

My Story About _____

By _____

Dinosaurs Mini Book

Materials

- Dinosaurs Mini Book patterns (pages 218 and 219)
- green or brown construction paper
- white paper
- scissors
- stapler

Assembly Directions

1. Copy pages 218 and 219 (one of each page per student) onto green or brown construction paper and cut out the dinosaur shapes to create the front and back covers of the Dinosaurs Mini Books.

2. Make copies of the dinosaur pattern (page 219) on white paper and cut them out to make the inside pages of the mini books. For early writers, two pages per book will probably be sufficient. For more experienced writers, increase the number of pages.

3. Assemble the books and staple them together.

Dinosaur Tracks Art Project

Materials

- white construction paper
- plastic dinosaurs
- several colors of tempera paint
- pie plates or other shallow containers

Preparation

- Put each color paint in a different shallow container and prepare for painting.

Assembly Directions

1. Show students how to dip the feet of the plastic dinosaurs into the paint and stamp "dinosaur tracks" onto the white construction paper.

2. Let students use different dinosaurs and different colors to make many tracks on their papers. They can make patterns with the different colors and foot shapes.

3. Encourage students to write stories about their dinosaur tracks.

Dinosaurs Mini Book

Cover

Dinosaurs Mini Book *(cont.)*

Back Cover and Inside Pages

Make **one** copy of this page.

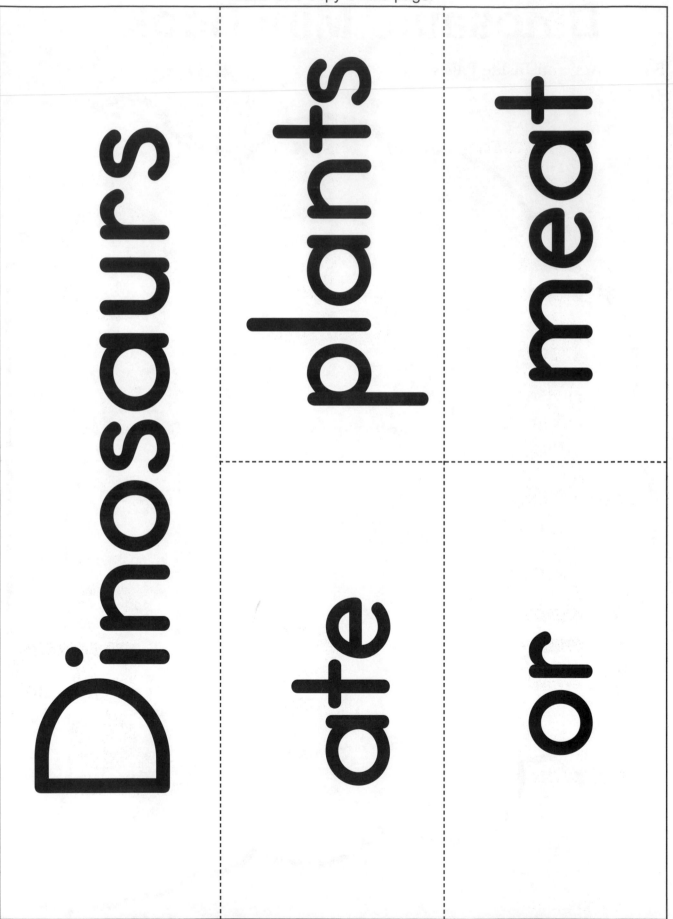

Make **one** copy of this page.

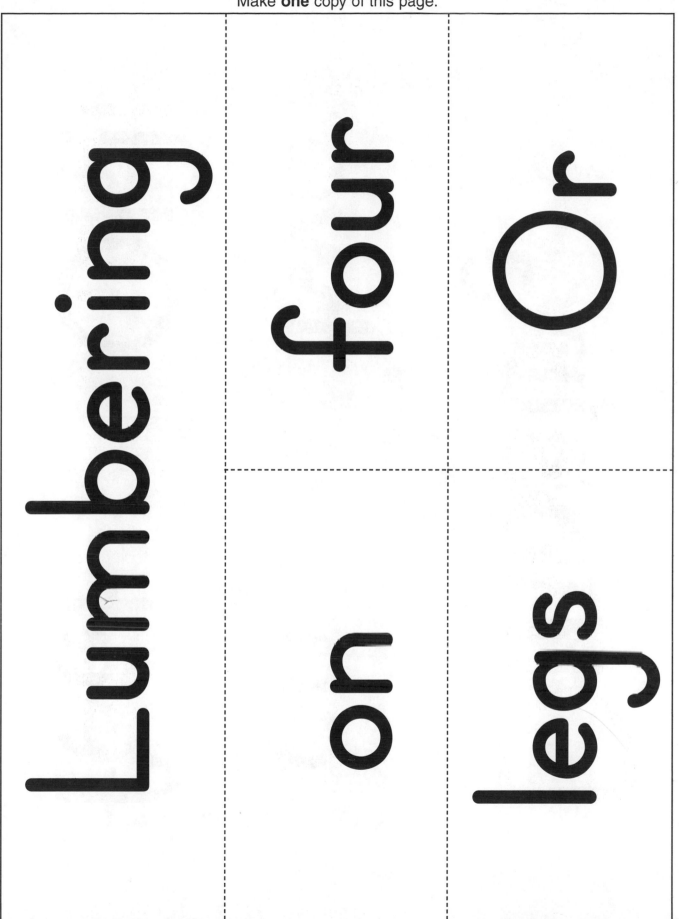

Lumbering

four

Or

on

legs

Make **one** copy of this page.

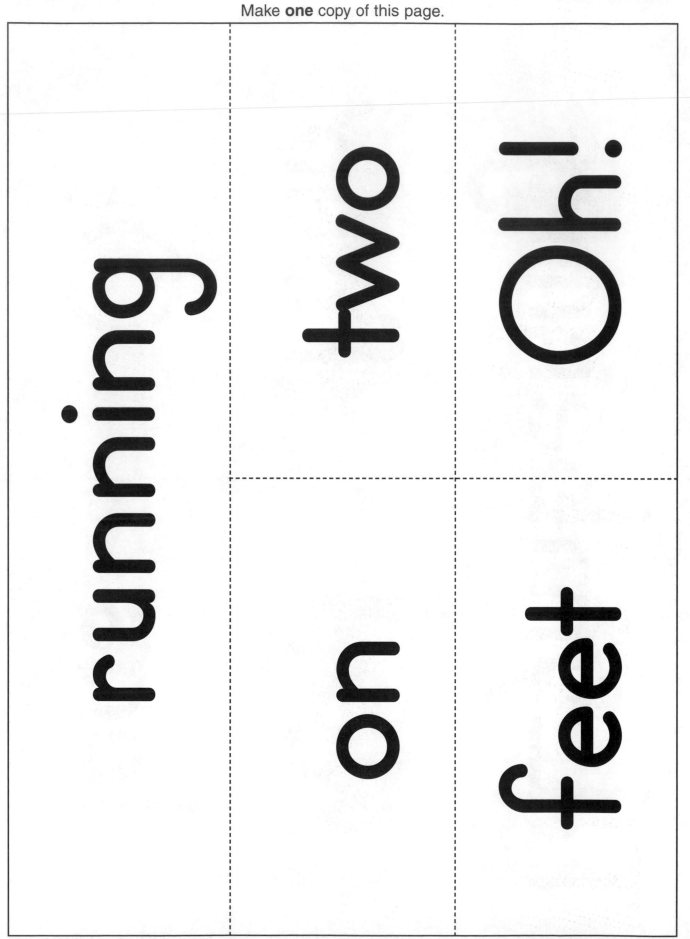

running

two

Oh!

on

feet

Make **one** copy of this page.

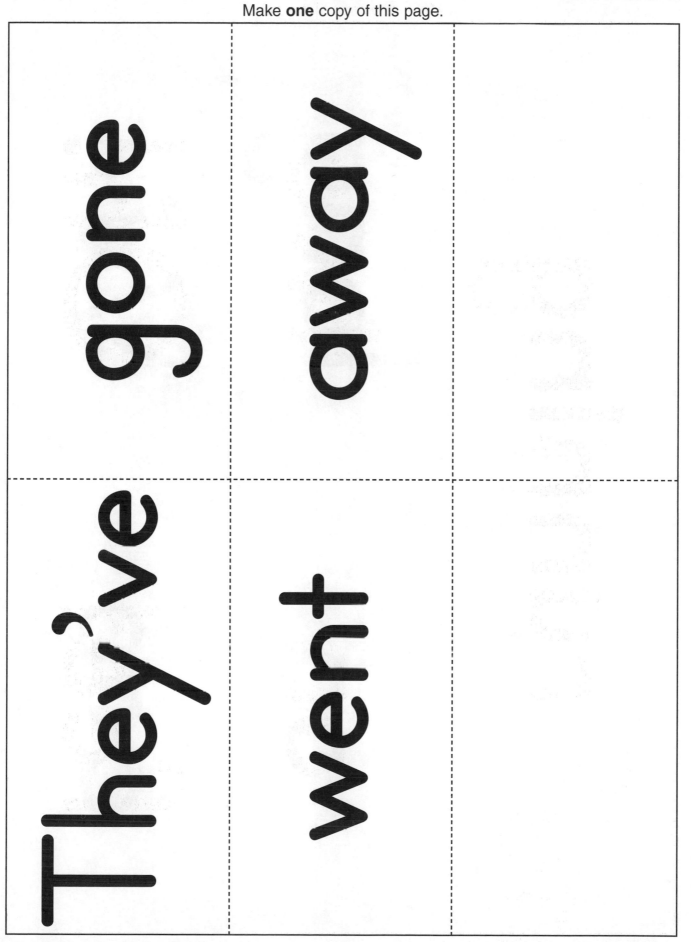

gone

away

They've

went

Make **one** copy of this page.

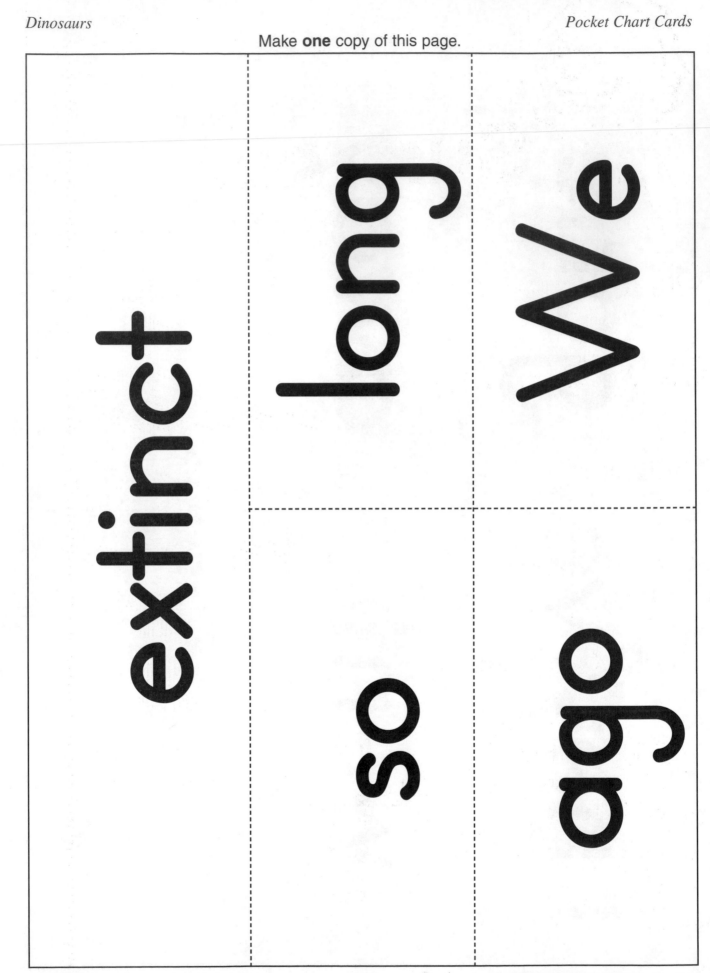

extinct

long

We

so

ago

Make **one** copy of this page.

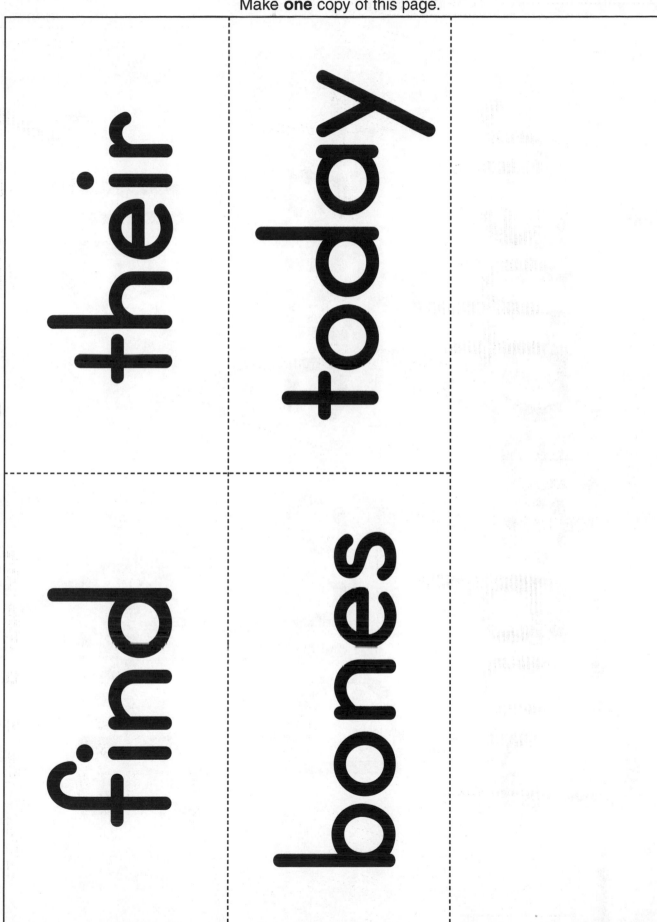

their

today

find

bones

Make **two** copies of this page.

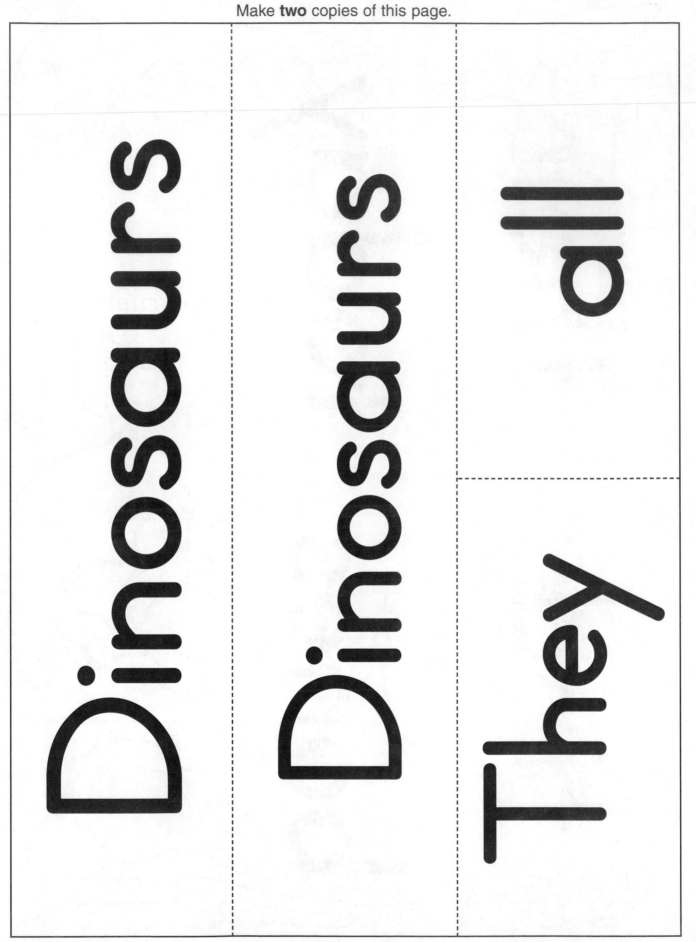

Dinosaurs

Dinosaurs

all

They

Sea Animals

(Sing to the tune of "Down by the Station")

Down in the water, the cool ocean water,

See the ocean creatures,

In their habitats.

Some live on the rocks and

Some swim in the water.

Some dig in the sand and

Some live on the shore.

Sea Animals

Materials

- age-appropriate fiction and nonfiction books about sea animals
- white board or chart paper and markers
- Sea Animals Song Pocket Chart Cards (pages 234–238) laminated and cut apart
- pocket chart
- markers, colored pencils, and crayons
- Sea Animals Story Writing Page for each child (page 229)
- assembled Sea Animals Mini Book for each student (pages 230–232)
- Sea Animal Patterns (page 233)
- Under the Sea project materials (page 233)

ocean

habitats

shore

Unit Introduction

1. Read a fictional story about sea animals. Discuss the setting, characters, and plot.

2. Share a nonfiction book about sea animals, pointing out interesting facts.

3. Brainstorm. Write *Sea Animals* at the top of a chart or white board. Ask students to share what they know about sea animals and write down their responses. Use the shared writing technique detailed on page 9.

4. Sing the Sea Animals song while pointing to each of the words on the pocket chart.

5. Pass out the Story Writing Page. Encourage students to write or draw their own stories about sea animals. You can use this time to do some guided writing with small groups or have the children write independently (see page 9).

6. Spend time with each child discussing his or her story or illustration. You will find tips for transcribing and editing students' stories on page 10.

Unit Activities

1. Continue sharing the fiction book about sea animals that you read during the unit introduction. Reread the nonfiction book and discuss interesting facts. Introduce additional books about sea animals during the week.

2. Add student ideas and new facts about sea animals to the brainstorming board.

3. Continue singing the Sea Animals song, pointing to the cards in the pocket chart each time. Remind students that they can use these words in their writing.

4. Use the Sea Animals Mini Book (pages 230–232) for guided or independent writing (see page 9). Encourage students to incorporate new information and ideas they have acquired since beginning the unit.

5. Complete the Under the Sea Art Project (pages 230 and 233). Display finished works in the classroom and encourage students to write about their art.

My Story About _____
By _____

Sea Animals Mini Book

Materials

- Sea Animals Mini Book patterns (pages 231 and 232)
- blue or gray construction paper
- white paper
- scissors
- stapler

Assembly Directions

1. Copy pages 231 and 232 (one of each page per student) onto blue or gray construction paper and cut out the whale shapes to create the front and back covers of the Sea Animals Mini Books.

2. Make copies of the whale pattern (page 232) on white paper and cut them out to make the inside pages of the mini books. For early writers, two pages per book will probably be sufficient. For more experienced writers, increase the number of pages.

3. Assemble the books and staple them together.

Under the Sea Art Project

Materials

- Sea Animal Patterns (page 233)
- large sheets of blue construction paper (one per student)
- sand or uncooked oatmeal
- small pebbles
- green tissue paper
- glue
- paint brushes
- scissors

Preparation

- Make copies of the Sea Animal Patterns (one page per student).

Assembly Directions

1. Give each student a large sheet of blue construction paper and show them how to spread glue on the bottom half of the paper using a paint brush. Help students sprinkle sand or oatmeal on the glue to create the sandy bottom of the ocean. They can add some pebbles to make rocks.

2. Show students how to tear or cut the green tissue and glue it on their papers to create seaweed.

3. Review ocean habitats (sandy bottom, rocks, seaweed, open water) and which animals live in each. Give each student a copy of the Sea Animals page. Let students color the animals, cut them out, and glue them into their ocean scene, placing them in the proper habitat.

4. Encourage students to write captions for or stories about their ocean scenes.

Sea Animals Mini Book

Cover

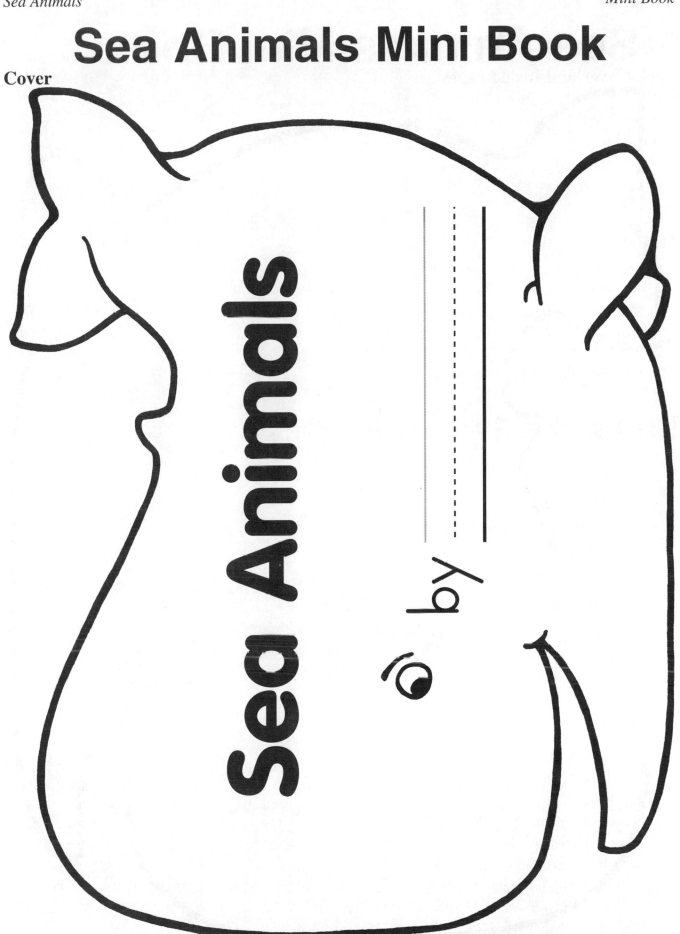

Sea Animals

© by

Sea Animals Mini Book *(cont.)*
Back Cover and Inside Pages

Sea Animals

Patterns

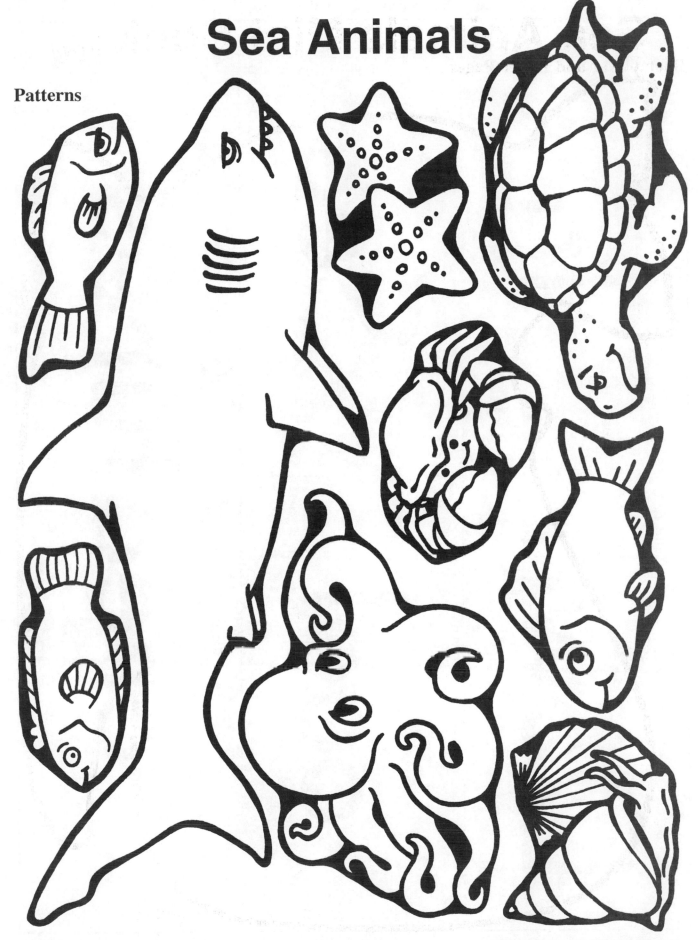

Make **one** copy of this page.

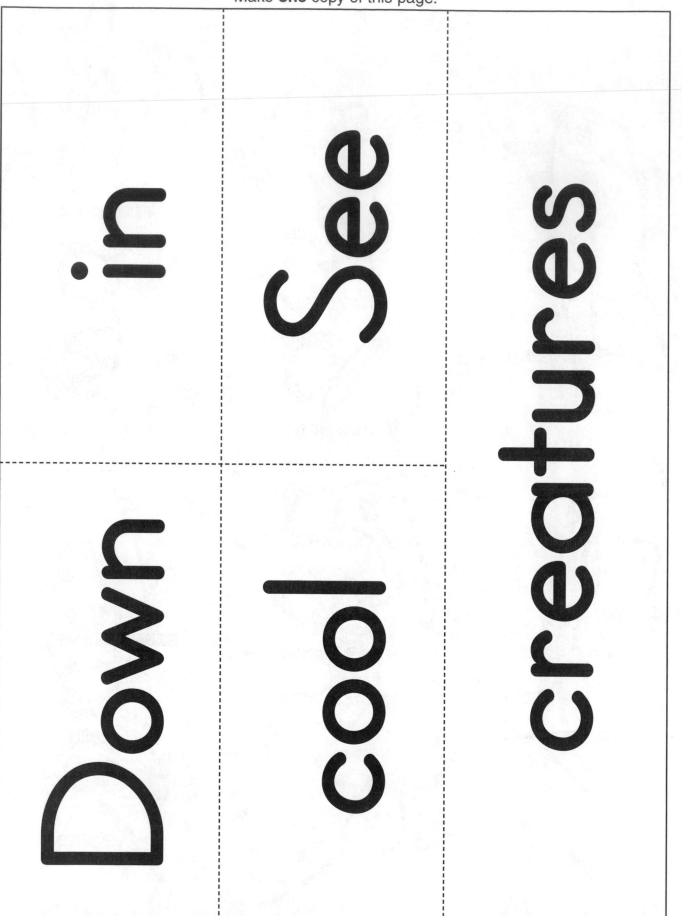

in

See

creatures

Down

cool

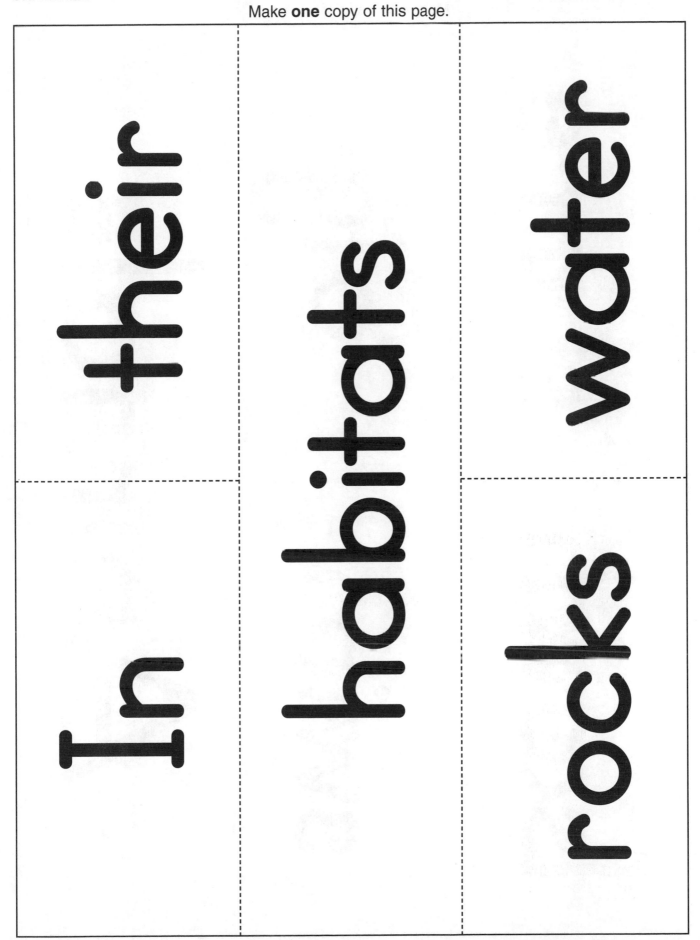

their

In

habitats

water

rocks

Make **one** copy of this page.

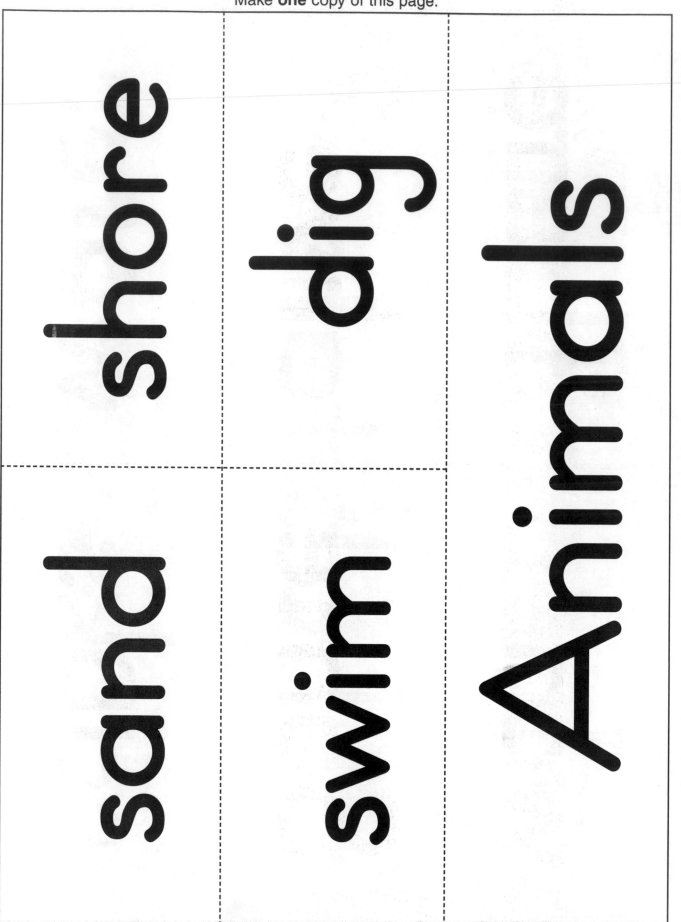

shore

dig

Animals

sand

swim

Make **two** copies of this page.

Some

live

on

water

Some

in

Make **two** copies of this page.

the

the

the

and

the

sea

ocean

Literature Suggestions

Fall
Fiction: Hall, Zoe. *Fall, Leaves, Fall!* Scholastic Inc., 1999.

Nonfiction: Maestro, Betsy. *Why Do Leaves Change Color?* Harper Trophy, 1994.

About Me
Fiction: Schlein, Miriam. *The Story About Me.* Albert Whitman and Company, 2004.

Nonfiction: Gainer, Cindy. *I'm Like You, You're Like Me.* Free Spirit Publishing, 1998.

Apples
Fiction: LeSeig, Theo (Theodor Geisel). *Ten Apples Up On Top.* Random House, 1998.

Nonfiction: Gibbons, Gail. *Apples.* Holiday House, 2000.

Community Helpers
Fiction: McPhail, David. *Pig Pig Gets a Job.* Dutton Books, 1990.

Nonfiction: Maynard, Christopher. *Jobs People Do.* DK Children, 1997.

The Moon
Fiction: Carle, Eric. *Papa Please Get the Moon for Me.* Little Simon, 1999.

Nonfiction: Gibbons, Gail. *The Moon Book.* Holiday House, 1997.

Winter
Fiction: Stewart, Paul. *A Little Bit of Winter.* HarperTrophy, 2000.

Nonfiction: Bancroft, Henrietta. *Animals in Winter.* Harper Trophy, 1997.

Friends
Fiction: Cohen, Miriam. *Will I Have a Friend?* BookWholesalers, 2002.

Nonfiction: Brown, Laurene Krasny. *How To Be a Friend.* Little, Brown, 1998.

Bears
Fiction: Wilson, Karma. *Bear Snores On.* Margaret K. McElderry, 2003.

Nonfiction: Bauer, Erwin and Peggy. *Bears of Alaska.* Sasquatch Books, 2002.

Stars
Fiction: Jeffers, Oliver. *How to Catch A Star.* Philomel Books, 2004.

Nonfiction: Mitton, Jacqueline. *Zoo in the Sky.* National Geographic Society, 1998.

Spring
Fiction: Walters, Catherine. *When Will It Be Spring?* Dutton Books, 2001.

Nonfiction: Fowler, Allan. *How Do You Know It's Spring?* Children's Press, 1992.

Farm Animals
Fiction: Cowley, Joy. *Mrs. Wishy-Washy's Farm.* Philomel, 2003.

Nonfiction: Jeunesse, Gallimard. *Farm Animals.* Scholastic, 1998.

Insects
Fiction: Laden, Nina. *Roberto, The Insect Architect.* Chronicle Books, 2000.

Nonfiction: Rockwell, Anne F. *Bugs Are Insects.* HarperTrophy, 2001.

Plants
Fiction: Silverstein, Shel. *The Giving Tree.* HarperCollins, 2004.

Nonfiction: Hickman, Pamela. *A Seed Grows.* Kids Can Press, 1997.

Weather
Fiction: Ford, Miela. *What Color Was the Sky Today?* Greenwillow, 1997.

Nonfiction: Simon, Seymour. *Weather.* Harper Trophy, 2000.

Summer
Fiction: Joosse, Barbara M. *Hot City.* Philomel Books, 2004.

Nonfiction: Klingel, Cynthia. *Summer.* Child's World, 2000.

Pets
Fiction: LaRochelle, David. *The Best Pet of All.* Dutton Children's Books, 2004.

Nonfiction: Watts, Claire. *Pets.* Two-Can Publishers, 2004.

Dinosaurs
Fiction: Nolan, Dennis. *Dinosaur Dream.* Aladdin, 1994.

Nonfiction: Aliki. *Digging Up Dinosaurs.* HarperTrophy, 1998.

Sea Animals
Fiction: Barner, Bob. *Fish Wish.* Holiday House, 2000.

Nonfiction: Earle, Sylvia. *Sea Critters.* National Geographic, 2000.

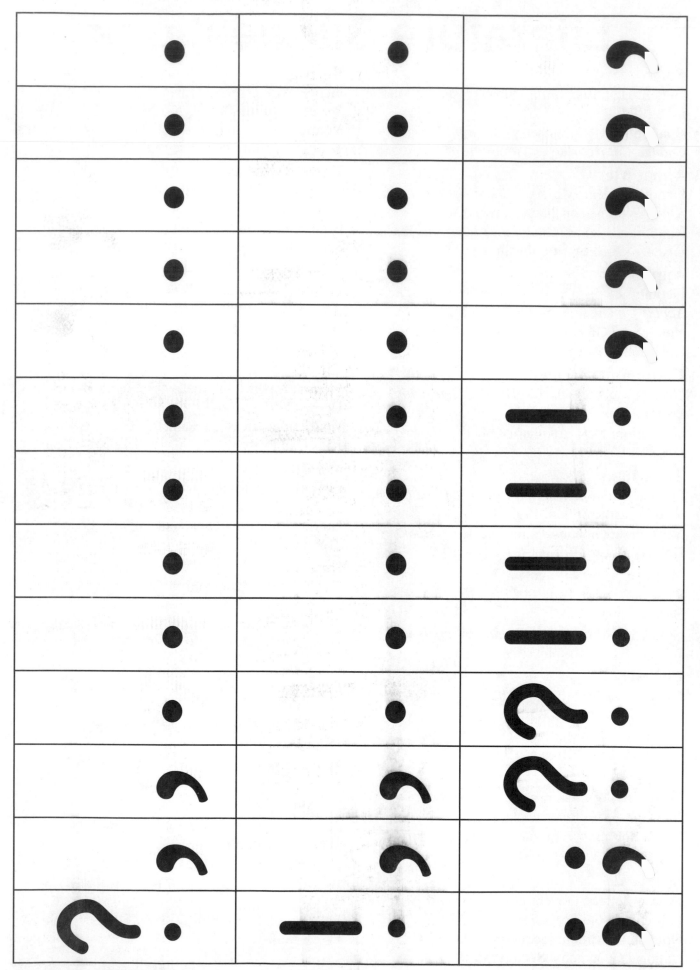